SE

G000149235

The Journey to Inner Peace
A Channelled Text

DANIEL MIRFIELD

New Earth Publishing
Melbourne, Australia
www.newearthpublishing.com

Copyright © 2022 Daniel Mirfield

ISBN 978-0-645-69651-6

A CIP catalogue record for this book is available from the National Library of Australia.

Edited and cover design by New Earth Publishing
Illustrations & front cover drawing by Mekala Rodrigo

DEDICATION

To every soul with whom I have exchanged experiences which led to a lifetime of learning, challenging, and encouraging me to follow my purpose of helping people around the world.

CONTENTS

ACKNOWLEDGMENTS

Writing this book was about committing and placing myself in a position where I could surrender and allow the knowledge and wisdom to be channelled. It has been recorded to help people access a natural way of healing. The channellings weren't as simple, or as easy as being told what to write. The way they presented the information was received by using a variety of different lines of communication. Some days I would let it flow through me, others I would see pictures and stories, or even translate a phrase or a saying into words, but above all else I had to open myself up to the pain of the world and allow an understanding of the deepest forms of healing.

Recognising there were so many different types of communication, I was aware early on that I needed someone with a creative gift, that could present a story through drawings. My publisher and good friend, Cristina Mullins, found an artist with a creative talent that resonated with the theme of what I was trying to achieve. Mekala Rodrigo has achieved great heights with her talent in drawing images that were described to her in words.

The book has layers upon layers of principles that will resonate with the energy of anyone, no matter what stage of the journey they are on. Mekala's drawings hold the frequencies of healing. When an individual looks at those drawings, they will see a story that will help them during the period of their life that the chapter represents.

We are constantly repositioning our stance during stages of healing. Take your time, be in that moment, understand that space within those pictures. When you're ready, a message or a knowing will be available. A story in of itself that was captured by the artist.

The dedication to healing spills over to everyone that has found themselves on a spiritual path and every soul that digests the book. The deepest form of healing is the individual's acceptance of their own accountability and acknowledgement that peace always comes from within.

I spent a lot of time alone, channelling and trying to best express the theme that was being presented to me. During times where I needed to ground or express my thoughts, Cristina was present to be a sounding board and friend. The way life is balanced, with the transfer of energy, allowed me to recognise and understand the messages I received about the divine feminine, by having both Mekala and Cristina contributing to the overall energy of the book.

This book could never be created by a masculine only lifeforce. By allowing that line of communication to filter through the divine feminine I was in turn balancing the book to the core principles of life. The power and strength of having friends that offer a space for you and respect boundaries, creates a divine understanding of friendship. Life has a far greater meaning when you have close friends to share these experiences with.

Seedling

The Journey to Inner Peace

CHAPTER 1

INTRODUCTION TO INNER PEACE

Throughout life we are faced with a variety of choices and decisions to make, creating different directions, leading to pathways that close and open many doors. This restricted reality will often create more questions than solutions or answers. Join me on this journey and we will talk about the spiritual connection to a oneness, a divine frequency that resonates with our soul's embodiment. We will identify a divine power that is lying inside of you. A power that can open new possibilities to a universal consciousness as it connects us to the planet and the universe. Within this book and during this journey we will outline truths where you can focus your attention inwards as the peace comes from within. I encourage everyone on this journey to access parts of themselves they haven't before.

Over the years society has divided and separated parts of us that connect us spirituality and scientifically. We will investigate the true meaning of why a spiritual lifestyle supported by science is the key component to an advanced, peaceful society. As we discuss key areas we will identify and recognise the true characteristics of our societal structure and see aspects of ourselves that have been created by design, while addressing patterning and energies that hold individuals in a state of fear and disconnection. As new generations are welcomed into the world, they are more likely to be faced with a structure that is dominated and controlled via technology. With the advancements of the last forty years, we can highlight changes to how society is reliant on technology and how our daily habits have changed, to continuously encourage us to disconnect from our purpose. A large amount of energy is discharged towards materialistic goals that will only ever control you and not support you. The way technology has targeted our minds creates a situation where mental health, psychological and physical issues arise. This will only get worse if we do not start moving towards a peaceful existence. Throughout this journey we will discuss areas of your life that will support you as you concentrate on your health and wellbeing, while gradually moving your soul towards enlightenment.

This book has been channelled and it made with the energy that while you are looking for answers within this book, I will be present as we walk along this path. Your identification starts by respecting yourself and being honest with who you are, identifying what motivated your past actions and how listening with an open mind is empowering. This is an honour which you deserve to give yourself. I welcome everyone to know that when times get hard you only need to look and see the sun shining through the clouds to know that you will never be alone, and the universe will support us. Allow yourself to release all the pain and anger in a way that requires you to be self-aware and accountable, while opening a space that welcomes love and harmony.

We have made life hard, and we create problems only to find the solutions and proclaim ourselves the victor, but never truly able to solve any of the genuine issues. This characteristic is relevant to our individual journey, as we continually neglect ourselves in support of a society and culture that shows we don't know who we really are. A lost soul, in a world that is dominated by wars, conflicts and greed. Over the last 10,000 years our shadows, which are controlled by fear, have resulted in painful and terrible actions that were undertaken by a dominant force which doesn't recognise your value when connecting in with your true alignment.

Hidden within the world, there are lifetimes of wisdom and ancient practices that have been ignored or removed from history. Society ignores sacred practices as they don't provide materialistic success for our modern world, and as we look towards your health, the key to this journey starts in the past. A past that formed your ideology and shaped your future, an insight that reviews how humans created so much pain. There are areas of our life where we have lost touch with vital lessons that were present within tribes and tribal stories, the caretakers that knew how to become part of the planet.

There is sacred knowledge that is hidden in your embodiment and by identifying yourself you can access all the necessary wisdom that is needed within this lifetime. The energy of that wisdom is readily available for you, you just need to start being honest with yourself. Your actions and thoughts need to resonate with the purity of your soul. Tribes and ancient settlements would look towards leaders like shamans, elders, gurus, and sages. These people would dedicate their life to nature, the planet, and the universe all in support of their tribe, while honouring the process and passing on all sacred knowledge and teachings. The tribal leaders that were in tune with their soul always knew it was not about them, but about everyone's individual journey on this planet. Not just humans but plants, animals, elements, and energies.

Your personal journey starts when you look inwards towards an ability that recognises that peace comes from within and by allowing a deeper connection to every aspect of your life, you can create spaces that are supported by an open mind. A space that helps healing during periods of evaluating different influential moments of your life. By grounding your reality, you will see the amount of knowledge that is readily available, a reality that has never been taught as we like to avoid our own happiness. Avoidance will only make the pain or situation worse. To help balance and allow yourself a moment of self-awareness I will guide you through key areas that influence your decision making and lifestyle choices. A time when kindness, loyalty, love, and empowerment will support and guide you as you grow into your embodiment, recognising yourself as an individual.

From the very first moment we are conditioned to act and display a personality that is designed to interact with narratives across all forms of society, while adapting as the narrative changes. Changes of rules and conditioning will directly affect your emotional, physiological, and physical energies. Displaying characteristics that are negatively driven by fear, anxiety, doubt, stress, envy, anger, lack of control, passive aggressiveness, and aggression. To spend a life that is experiencing all those emotions daily is a life not lived. I encourage you to take those experiences and allow them to make you stronger, attract and bring love into a period that disconnects you. Heal yourself and allow your journey to inspire and support others in times of darkness.

The designed structure of our current way of life allows you to remove and ignore all accountability. A disconnected reality shows us that during times of hardship, as we encounter demanding situations it is easier to do the wrong thing, than to do the right thing. As we move through the book, allow an open mind that understands self-awareness and being accountable for your life, the foundations of your thoughts and actions starts and stops with you. Your choices and actions are a display of how you want the world to see you. The parts of your life that need healing will only truly begin to heal when your self-awareness makes you accountable for your personal journey within this life. There is no one else on this planet that is the same as you, your journey is specialised and unique to your own identity.

Throughout any stages of healing, enlightenment and awakening an open mind knows the value of kindness and caring attitude towards yourself and those that are close to us. There are parts of this book that will only reveal the answer when you're ready to listen. The pain that the world has been subjected to will not heal overnight, it is a slow and emotional journey. Respect is required across all stages of healing and to be witness to someone else's actions when they are at a different stage of their journey will be one of your first tests, as your strength is measured by the reaction of your character, an empowerment that knows boundaries and displays a kind and respectful manner. I encourage you to take notes and discuss all areas of this book, allowing an empowerment that resonates to the higher knowledge and tender loving care of your embodiment.

To some the world may feel small and to others they may feel closed off. Self-love and allowing your heart to guide you needs time, and time will always be on your side when you are ready to be in the moment. Patience is a term that causes more pain, removing the understanding if the wisdom it obtains. By acknowledging your personal journey, when doors open and close, patience and self-awareness will be required to see the whole picture.

Throughout any stage of healing and self-reflection we are faced with decisions that were previously ignored. For now, just asking the right questions will help in taking the correct steps forward. With every step forward know that there's a lesson that will help you evolve, while adapting to making key decisions. At times life will become hard, know that it's a strength to seek help and guidance. Little acts of kindness within a single moment can change your approach and mindset. Allow the healing and an unconditional approach to a loving caring formula that will support you. Know that within this moment, the moment your eyes run over the words, is the same exact time it is divinely connected for you to look inwards so you can look outwards. Knowing that you are meant to be here and that a sacred space has been opened just for you to truly honour and heal yourself. A guidance that is part of you which helps you understand the energies that complete you.

We open and close sacred spaces throughout our day and the energy I put into this book will be received in a unique and different way for everyone involved. The energy that is held, asks you to be honest with yourself and others, being truthful to your journey and the world we live in will open stages of healing as you move towards inner peace. An honest platform that creates a stable ground to fulfil your true life's purpose.

The energy of the book holds the qualities of self-awareness, self-love, and enlightenment, and with those energies the vision of a divine alignment with your soul is created from inside your heart space. It is within your own essence to control your empowerment, embrace this beautiful journey and walk along the path that resonates and recognises who you truly are.

At this point take five minutes for yourself to create a calm environment, ground yourself and call in the energy to help you attract the knowledge you require that synchronises with your collective frequencies and your vibrational alignments. As you find a comfortable and calm place, close your eyes, and envision a white room. Within this room there is a large, old, hand-carved door. This door has no handle nor lock, it opens when your mind acknowledges its unconditional beauty and wisdom. You approach the door and ask it to open. Within your state of self-reflection, it does so and reveals a pathway surrounded with trees that displays the silhouetted features of nature that creating a path. As you move forward and look at the path you realise there are hands that are imprinted across different surfaces, which are highlighted by a low glow. You instinctively understand that it is an acknowledgement of all the souls that have travelled along this journey before you, knowing within this moment you are not alone. In fact, the energy holds a great understanding of power and wisdom which you could gain within this place of enlightenment. A voice in your mind speaks up and reminds you that even though you are not alone on this journey, it is only you that is responsible for your actions, thoughts, and wellness. You're entitled to find peace in this lifetime.

As we move through the book, you will realise how important it is to open and close sacred spaces. I will ask you to question all areas and use your life experiences as a reference. Give yourself permission and time to process them properly. The ironic thing is that we already have all the answers inside of us, it's about being able to access them. The lessons and teaching within this journey will ask for you to recognise your heart space and keep an open mind. This allows you to look at a different way of thinking while evaluating the world around you. A journey towards your inner peace, fulfilling your soul's contract and embracing the honour we have in this life.

CHAPTER 2

EMOTIONS AND FEELINGS

With every heartbeat, a stroke of a brush adds to the painting of life. As the painting evolves with every individual experience, no limits are placed on the scale of completion. An open mindset may draw upon the reality that constant growth is necessary for the picture. A picture that you will only be able to see completed, with the honour of standing back and reflecting once time does not exist. Our current lives are scales to be measured. A calculated conclusion of a risk assessment, valued on how we participate and stabilise events while cementing our place and our purpose within society.

A new life is everything, and yet there is no guaranteed way in which you will react when looking upon a new life as you gaze into each other's eyes for the first time. Feelings that can't be truly expressed in any language across the world. The painting in which your life has been designed and manipulated through years of conditioning is left behind. Although they have dedicated their lives to a purpose that supports the structure of society's ideologies, their heartbeat within this single moment have now changed the style of the way your brush paints.

The growth of a new soul attaching to their embodiment is about to undertake the journey of a set of cards, and depending on their family, a predetermined reality of who they are is about to be drawn. Growing up we learn how to pick ourselves up, the values of laughing walk lockstep in line with the values of crying, a conditioned platform as we are open to all life lessons. Lessons that as we grow, our parents or guardians will explain, teach, and express every stage of growth as you evolve into your body. The painting in which your life exists is now forming your personality traits, a character that has been taught life lessons now understands the trajectory their life will be subjected to, while carving out the canvas of the reality in how they participate across society.

For the world to exist under the umbrella it currently functions, a life painting will only ever be understood after the completion of this life. A timeless place where accountability and responsibility does not exist. The conditions in which those traits are required are placed upon the soul and its embodiment. A spiritual life is linked to the divine light and works beyond the logical conclusion of existence. The silhouette in which your hand expresses, from a distance, confuses the eye in how it acknowledges and interprets the way it sees others. An untrained eye will blur out the silhouette and avoid the details within the imprint of the finger. The details are the experiences that are part of us, as we learn to guide our way through life, faced with the constant transfer of energies across conversations. Our ideology is now built on the teachings of our beliefs. From making friends, playing sports, learning to dance, getting your first job, all moments that are part of the heartbeat that you continue to paint.

The way you transfer the energy and receive it from others can either enlighten you or restrict the flow of energy that stumps the personal growth of identity. Growing up we blindly place our faith in those that look after us, with no reason for doubt or to question the life experiences of others. Free will and choice is available in every moment, a reality that is ignored as conditioned ideologies are placed upon the forefront of your mind. The healing of an individual all starts with feelings and emotions, as a part of your life that opens doors to the collective consciousness of the universe.

Feelings and emotions cannot be taught, it is a part of you that only provides the answer when you search from within. A troubled mind does not know the value of what an unconditional space holds, it is the divine timing of being timeless. A part of the painting that cannot be seen through the eye of a logical mind. As you move forward in search of finding a part of you that resonates with a peaceful moment, you soon question your actions and if your interpretation of the world is seen through the lens of your eyes or someone else's vision. A blurred vision has never offered a space of self-care, only to be burdened by the past and the reality of a troubled society that fails to identify individual souls.

Terminology is presented in a manner that focuses on pain, removing the boundaries that fails to provide a space.

The interchangeable actions of a belief that are projected towards an individual can restrict and close the mind, by shutting doors. As the default internal conflicts dominate the conversation. A brush stroke that is now painting the life of someone else. Avoidance by design, removes the ability of understanding the value of your life.

Feelings and emotions are a gateway to a wholeness, a divine life principle in knowing that your own life is and always will be unique. With feelings and emotions comes recognizing the identity within the individual and as an individual you are now enlightened by the task of actions that resonate with your soul. A place that holds a disconnected reality hides away in fear of reviewing past actions and blocks all avenues to avoid being accountable while surrendering your own happiness. You cannot teach someone the values of their life, if you're trying to live it for them, a controlling behaviour that mimics the aura of how society functions.

Defining your feelings has never been about the academic space between you and a book, it is a knowing that is found from looking beyond. Beyond the space of acceptance, shapes your future on not only how you see yourself but how you participate and interact within society. What it truly means to express yourself in a manner that resonates with your soul, is connected to knowing who you are. Modern day society has created a way of life where you can easily glide through the years, actively avoiding your true purpose.

Time is the beauty of life that will only ever be on its own clock, an area of our life that we can't control, nor should we fight. A deeper connection to a higher knowing is about being in the moment and embracing the journey that is present. A greater understanding that all types of lessons learnt is accessing the wisdom within each moment, connecting our embodiment to a wholeness. Every moment that involves a period of self-awareness when reflecting on our feelings, or periods of time that we are faced with a rush of emotions, can either make us stronger with a deeper alignment or form a disconnected reality. A concept that is rarely explained nor taught, avoided, and removed in a reality that pulls you away from your individualised purpose within this lifetime. Time isn't just relevant to emotions and feelings, it's a core understanding of how we empower our freedom.

A purpose that isn't bound by greed and restrictions, only to create a connection that allows you to follow a natural direction that aligns with your soul's contract. The concept of a higher knowing is achieved when a space is presented, allowing the internal collective frequency to communicate to places beyond what your eyes can see. How the transfer of feelings and emotions are displayed can result in a creative outlet that matches the frequencies of how you felt, and not all feelings are expressed in words. Frequencies are connected to a divine language, as it allows feelings to flow freely through us. The entire process of understanding our embodiment can be very unnatural when placed upon restrictions, it requires nurturing and patience, two qualities that go against the grain in which you may potentially operate.

Our terminology and definition of explaining the basic principles of feelings and emotions are limited to the fact that we do not have a clue, a place to avoid in a concept that releases all self-empowerment. The painting in which your life was subjected to, started clean, as a blank canvas, and surrounding that canvas is a picture frame. A limited reality of what you can achieve within this lifetime, when we look at allowing the free-flowing energies of feelings and emotions, it is beyond the world of which the frame has contained.

To honour the whole embodiment and your journey within this life starts with understanding that the canvas of your painting works beyond a two-dimensional plane and has no limit to how far the expansion of consciousness can flow. Feelings and emotions have been limited to achieve control, but the purpose of this life is about embracing the powers that involve dedicating a loving relationship with your identity, as you use a reference point of your heartbeat.

Our physical traits within our embodiment are the start of building a relationship towards acknowledgement. Our feelings and emotions are linked to all physical aspects across the planet. We access them by honouring ourselves in a place of self-awareness and we are born with gifts that have become restricted by design. They are restricted to fulfil the basic conditions of society. These gifts are hearing, seeing, smelling, tasting, and feeling. They have a bond that needs to be reconnected to allow the flow of an organic set of communications. Restricting these natural gifts, will close the mind as you have relayed a message of avoidance, forcing an unnatural reaction that can display traits of anger, stress, anxiety, and fear. The reaction in which you select your conclusion can be in some cases predetermined. If you choose the outcome and there is an alternative that shows signs of accountability or responsibility it is easier to avoid and blame than embrace. The choice of choosing to see the outcome is forcing you to step away from honouring a place of enlightenment. Your place of peace has never been about controlling yourself or others but understanding that self-care is freedom when listening to the heartbeat of life.

An exchange of conversation is only limited to the limits you place upon yourself, a closed reality is selecting what they want to hear. A habit that has reduced the way in how you operate across all exchanges of energy transfers. It is the place of self-awareness that acknowledges the process of accountability, in which it understands the importance of an open mind, and it works outside the parameters of a conditioned reality. The procedure in which the mind digests the reaction from an activation of your gifts, will indicate the strength of your mind and the type of internal response. Avoidance of your gifts will be drawn to an addictive state, targeting a response in an emotionally charged way. The uncontrollable actions that follow, displays a mindset that shows your response and lack of emotional control.

When you don't identify the true value of using your ability to connect to the world beyond, it numbs the appreciation of participating in your own life. Default reactions of avoidance and addictions soon control the way you reject any other outcome but your own pain. Feelings and emotions, natural abilities that are forever changing and evolving across the consciousness of the universe, restricting the space to a framework can only truly survive if you remove any ability to appreciate the world around you. If you see pain, you will experience it, shifting your attention to addictive items that fill an emotional state like phones, food and aggression are all symptoms of ignoring and shutting down.

It is not the picture frame that you fear, it is the shadow of your own life that has been blocked like a hurricane, circling around with nowhere to escape. The truth is a small percentage of reactions in which you escalate to an uncontrollable point, as the mind struggles to understand the constant influx of emotions that are charging you and causing a fight or flight survival mode. By pushing the truth of your feelings and emotions aside and burying them deep inside of you, other painful past experiences dominate your reality. It is the truth within the shadow you seek to heal.

Restrictive mindsets create a narrative where we will consistently fill our daily routines to maximise our productivity as we aim to be as efficient as possible. This efficiency is to avoid the period where you are left alone with your own mind and will only start the hurricane that circulates with no place to go. We avoid ourselves as we try to remove any relationship and get out of our own head. When failing to understand who you are can mean that your healing is never available, as you fear the very thought of being in your own mind. It is the relationship of activating and acknowledging your gifts, while building a loving relationship with yourself that will lead to the embodiment of truth.

Throughout a spiritual transformation of the birth of your true self we must actively recognise all aspects and energies that are present when we are reviewing our own feelings and emotions. Any period of self-awareness can be difficult. The idea of changing habits and ideologies that affect your own perception can be a very emotional time, encountering a lot of hard truths that need to be addressed. We can start by defining the difference between feelings and emotions. This concept is told by a story and over the next few pages I ask you to relate through the experience of how you are currently using your gifts and registering if you're in control of your own feelings.

As any story begins, we have a journey, a journey that involves the teachings of two separate experiences. The first story begins in early spring, blessed by the change of weather, the start of this day was like any other, a clear blue sky and a view as far as your eyes can see. A person journeying along the side of a mountain approaches a river. From first glance the river is calm and holds a gentle stream flowing casually down the mountain side. Able to see the rough depth of the river they choose to cross, while for a moment stopping and standing in the middle of the stream, observing the world from a distinct perspective. For in this moment everything is new, and they are intrigued by what their eyes were registering. Distracted by time and unaware of their surroundings, a storm from the other side of the mountain has caused a rapid increase of water that the river now carries. The volume of water is approaching an uncontrollable speed and power. Hesitation and indecisiveness have spread through their mind into how to leave the riverbed, only to see they've slipped while scrambling to try and hold on, to stop the water from taking them downstream. Eventually losing grip and being taken with the water downstream. The battle of fighting against the water is hard, tiring and drains all their physical and mental strength. The river is full of debris and sharp objects, the battle to fight the river while trying to avoid being hurt is long and drawn out. They are eventually washed up on a river bank a long way downstream. Contemplating and angry, kicking themselves that they could have done things differently, but still totally unaware of their surroundings. An experience that has limited their approach to life and crossing bodies of water, drawing on fears and anxiety of past events when making future decisions. They now find themselves in a place that is unknown and forget about their original journey, in the hope they will survive.

In the second story a new day begins where a different person decides to follow the mountain path, blessed by blue skies and the sun shining, they can hear nature in its vibrant beauty. Soon they come across the same river, reviewing the crossing they notice several different energies that are present. A herd of deer are drinking from across the riverbank, the sound of the water making its way down the hill, the taste of spring in the air as the wind makes its way through the trees and across the mountain side. They notice that the riverbed has smooth rocks, surrounded by sand and after deciding to cross the person takes off their shoes and makes their way to the other side. Feeling the temperature of the water, the softness of sand and the smooth surfaces of the stones. Aware of solid and secure places to stand, while hearing the birds that fly overhead, talking between themselves. As the person reaches halfway, they notice the change in temperature, the deer and birds have either gone or quietened down, the flow of the water has changed slightly, and they can see dark clouds slowly making their way over from the other side of the mountain. Detecting a change of smell in the air, they decide to make it to safe ground and get to the other side of the river. When they reach the far riverbank, they see that a heavy increase of the speed and volume of water has become powerful and uncontrollable. Moving towards a large tree to get out of the oncoming rain they notice the animals taking cover in the bushes. The wind has stopped, the noise of the water is louder and drawing with it a coldness. Feeling the grass and the temperature of the ground before taking a moment to live in the experience of nature. Noticing that with all these sudden changes there is a calmness in the air, a higher point of reflection.

By putting yourself in a position to experience emotions from a different point of view allows you to experience the true power and qualities of a moment that is filled with emotions. During this lifetime, you are here to be part of the experience when faced with the energies of emotions.

Emotions allow you to embrace your own personal journey. Not letting internal and external emotions overpower you is challenging, as a lack of control will take you places where you are constantly fighting for survival. To be able to view how the water made its way through the land while acknowledging the elements around you is the power of being able to be in the moment. Being in the moment, is witnessing nature at its purest, all elements and divine energies combine to form a sacred power that is only experienced in an enlightened embodiment.

The time frames of both people were constant in each event, but how you spend your time, respecting the gifts that you have will only enhance your ability to touch deeper inside of you for a true alignment. We spend most of our lives ignoring and disconnecting from what is available to us while allowing emotions to control our daily patterns. This will shut down and minimise our natural sensors, just like the first person in the story, only seeing the obvious, enough to survive in an emotionally charged state of disconnection. The way the individual used their gifts in the story is merely the beginning of what humans are capable of. There are layers upon layers of abilities that are available, but this starts with you and humanity finding inner peace.

Explaining important aspects of your life can be hard to digest or understand. The idea of a concept that doesn't quite synchronise can create blockages. Here's an example of how to understand the ways in which emotions remove and control you, and the ways you should be embracing all experiences. During a wedding it is filled with emotions.

On the special day one of the dominant forces that drives everyone is emotions. This is a time of celebration where a variety of people come together to share their love and gratitude when a couple chooses to affirm and strengthen their love for each other. The idea of the couple can have a different effect on everyone, all depending on their personal life and past experiences. It's how you handle the happiness and love of two people internally. An emotionally charged person that has struggled to understand past events may draw conclusions that they're lonely, and lack love and strength, drawing on characteristics of envy and jealousy, while also making the day about themselves. Never truly understanding the real reason they were there in the first place. Emotions that have removed you from being in the moment, only shower you in negativity and passive self-identity issues. Issues that may not just occur on the day, but for many days, weeks and months later. You may find yourself in a period where you feel lost and entangled in an emotionally charged state.

Whereas, like the second person in the story, an event like this was never about them, it was about being present and witnessing a couple sharing their love in front of friends and family, registering the energy and commitment that each other share. To be in the moment allows a time where energies can change, evolve, grow, and affirm a power that lies inside of you. The power of knowing that listening and using your gifts in a moment that has nothing to do with you, but that you are honoured to be a part of the day. This guides you with love, care and wisdom in a world that can sometimes hide the true meaning of life.

Emotions are unpredictable and when left unchecked they are uncontrollable. Filling people with so many negative fears that it's easy for them to lose track of their true identity. Understanding your emotions will help you gain a greater knowledge of knowing which energies lie deep inside of you. If ignored they will block the way for you to welcome in positive and loving emotions. The way feelings and emotions are interpreted can influence the way you are using your ability to connect with the rest of your embodiment, and the chances are you could be using them the wrong way round. Reacting on emotions and minimising your feelings, creates a state of adrenaline that dominates your reactive consciousness to restrict any alternative lines of communications.

When you shut off the use of your feelings, as the influential energies of emotions push away any internal ability to accept their true purpose, they will be reversed to target addictive states that are controlled by your emotions. This applies to every gift that you're ignoring. Knowing that your feelings have been that heavily ignored, you are now using their purpose to encourage your emotions to close off your mind.

Emotions are available to be a witness of all blessings that one can experience within this life. If you let emotions take you places that you don't want to go, it will be a constant struggle, as the more you fight with emotions, the further away you get from understanding their true beauty. Fighting emotions leads to repetition of behavioural patterns, repeating the same problem over and over again. Not accepting the lessons, but only digging deeper. An addictive state of ignorance to justify your behavioural patterns is a tough place to accept any type of change. An unconditional space, to allow people the gratitude of self-healing and breakdown old mental traumas is a place that the world needs right now.

Feelings should always be allowed to receive the energetic messages of your surroundings, using your gifts to understand the lessons of growth as you're evolving into your embodiment. We struggle with the value of an open mind. Your sight and the visionary conclusion will be a challenge that most people will have. As you start to learn the negative reactions of judgement, it will highlight a huge influential shackle on how you interpret the world. A reality formed by a lack of identity across all different energies and spaces manipulate your state of mind and triggers emotions to shut down any welcome messages.

CHAPTER 3

ENERGY

The energetic transfer that shapes the circle of life, is the growth of a seedling that cannot be contained. A language of a divine principle that allows a soul to experience the meaning of life within this universe. The lessons of life are only limited to the freedoms within the mind. This is an energy in which a reality will determine how much of this life is blessed and ready to blossom, or is placed upon restrictions, only for other external energies to look upon their constraints. The window of reflection is always difficult to look upon, especially those that have been placed with restrictions and limitations, struggling to understand the workings of their mind.

The suggested idea of getting out of your own mind is advice that pushes mental health issues deep inside, only to be triggered later. The avoidance of your thoughts creates blockages for all external free flowing energies, rejecting the welcome insights while diverting and repelling their purpose. This results in the mind failing to understand the event, pushing their reality to a place of turbulence and conflict. Showing symptoms of engaging in an internal battle only to limit their vision to a storm. It looks like one, feels like one, but never climatises nor dissipates. It's a constant attack that circulates around the mind with no relief.

The transfer of energy is the enlightenment of your heartbeat. Every communication, interaction, event, and experience are sustained by the transfer that is forever changing, adapting, and evolving. Placing ourselves in the framework of a logical reality, restricts and minimises the growth of your existence, removing the flow of energy and disregards the stable quality of a balanced universe.

Feelings and emotions exist in the world outside of the framework that society has created for a conditioned reality. The energy that flows naturally as it understands the unique direction in which the lines of communication harmonise to the abundant growth around the planet. A place of healing will require you to break that glass ceiling and embrace the circle of life, a concept that focuses our attention to look upon the tree of life. There is no way for a compromised seedling to understand the advanced network of communications that carry the wisdom linked to the divine source. Our inability to identify the freedom within our own minds, struggles with the simple acknowledgement that you're trapped. A trapped mind is a place where the energies are unable to enlighten a space, even for a moment, to reflect on your current status.

The tree of a life grows strong and tall when the roots are deep and connected to a network that allows the constant interaction of exchangeable energies. These energies provide the reference point aligned with freedom.

The roots are what stabilise the growth and strength of the tree. It supplies additional support during environmental conditions that affect everything on the surface. Inside you is the seedling of your own life, and the roots represent your ability to walk in your own shadow without it overpowering and forcing you to surrender in fear of what hides in the dark. There is an internal light that is linked to the conduit of enlightenment.

By facing your fears and accepting the transition to the collective consciousness of your mind, is the acknowledgment of walking with your internal light towards the dark of your own shadow. Knowing that welcoming the energies of life will show you that what is hidden in the darkness can remove the controlling, addictive states of your mind trying to play games and preventing you from accessing the truth. The truth, once accepted, will always allow the energies of the universe to flow freely through you.

What is hidden in the dark is always escalated by the constant attack and overreach of external forces. It survives on your ability to stay within your limitations. Imagine this hurricane circulating around your mind, while the influential attachments of external forces are continuing to stir the pot of emotions until it's ready to boil over. There is no release. The instant shutdown of the mind as it crawls in search of avoidance, only to be presented with an avenue of moving towards a programmed format. This creates an environment to escape the need to identify your own feelings and emotions. You are halting the flow of which allows you to digest events and process all environmental conditions. However, with energy it doesn't just stop, it is forever moving, and you are now left with the burden of what energies are available to you. The constant circulating around the whole of your mind and body has created a new theme of fear.

We are now approaching an energetic transfer that seeks to rebalance the world. An unconditional space is required to heal the deepest of wounds. The evolutionary pathways of humanity and science are now faced with the karmic balances of past events. These events have created negative abnormalities through a constructed design that seeks to destroy. Breaking through that barrier is difficult, especially when you've surrounded yourself with energies that hold you in a state of pain. The value of a soul that looks on, knows that the deepest form of healing is not an action they can say or do, but to offer a space. When a light shines over the restricted border of your ideology, it is like the sun shining through the clouds and allowing you to see the light.

Unconditional spaces of energy are clean and pure, a blessing for within that moment it can help a person see the awakening of a sunrise. The light that has always been present and available when you look within. It is the relationship of your feelings and emotions that connects the mind to a deeper part of your internal self. The shadow which your mind has avoided holds a deeper meaning of expansiveness, a place where once you have accepted that you've sabotaged yourself, a higher knowledge of wisdom is available at the other side of the shadow. A door that accesses an unlimited collective network of enlightenment is waiting at the other side. The knowing of accepting that peace comes from within.

Your mind and how it interprets the processing of thoughts will be limited by what you are willing to accept, and a lack of personal control can restrict the reality in which the images are drawn. What hides in the dark is the truth, and it's not the dark that you fear, but the disconnected reality of how your mind fails to understand the basic flow of energies. The conflict in which your mind creates narratives and circulates the outcomes is supported by the conditioned fear of not knowing how to be at peace in your own company. This is all part of acknowledging that your growth has been contained. It has been targeted so your mental ability in situations means you are unable to understand anything outside of your reality. The dark is a myth, it is the fear that you place upon yourself that stops the growth of your happiness by limiting your purpose within the borders of the frame.

The tree of life grows with the roots of freedom, a place of grounding as the collective network of the planet produces the cycle of life. Your strength is the connection from within your mind that can honour the space that is hidden in the darkness, and then you'll understand the reasons why freedom has been hidden from you. The energy in which you seek to free yourself, moves away from the compounds in which your reality has been locked. The release of short-sighted burdens is to look from within, by travelling to an unknown place along the mountain range it allows you to look upon your blessings.

Your life's interpretation of a divine existence is supported by the energies that ground your reality and allow you bring your attention back to a place of self-awareness. Society has complicated controlling narratives that project and attack with enormous amounts of unnatural energy. Individuals fail to process the source that consumes them. There is no space or available access to a grounding source, to acknowledge a freedom that one needs to reflect on their actions. Digesting someone else's energy soon becomes a harsh reality of their visual breakdown, as the energy in which someone has forced upon them now becomes part of the mind. This is a constructed interpretation when selecting and ignoring how to process daily interactions and events. A painful accumulation of a build-up that transfers energy as it continuously jumps from one to the next. A reality in someone's mind that has gained momentum now surges through the internal workings of people that fail to recognise and release the controlling energies.

The storm that was circulating around someone's mind has now been projected as large amounts of people are subjected to these conditions. As they struggle with the internal battle, they release all empowerment and are open to suggestive ideas. A mind that just wants to be free but ends up giving away all their power in a moment as they struggle to understand the constant attack of projected energies.

The state of disempowerment is locking someone in their own mind, while gradually adding fuel to the fire until

the controlling agenda is ready to show its cards. Any person or community that has been subject to an alternative motive, will be placed upon a reality that either distracts their attention or removes their ability to see the motive. The shackled chains that remove your freedom in an objective for someone to gain power, a set of circumstances that gain momentum across all thunderstorms merging into an uncontrollable and unidentified transfer of energy.

Personal anger and lack of freedom encourages people to send expressions of pain and messages that aim to target the weakness in individuals that struggle to identify the relationship of their mind, body, and soul. The nature in which the transfer of energy has been created and influenced by the source, will either enlighten your empowerment or disempower you and remove your identity.

As you move forward in life, the topic of transferred energy will be one that you keep close to your heart. A sacred door that opens your world to a life beyond the constraints of the manufactured reality. The tree of life knows that the strength of the roots supports the structure in which it blossoms. A forever changing atmosphere of integrated forces that support the environment is how it achieves great heights. Throughout all weather conditions and seasons it knows the wisdom that is available by being present and adapting to work with the qualities of nature. Once it has accepted the place of freedom and has broken through the surface layer of the ground, it is now open and heading towards the most vulnerable stage of its life. Stages of growth that are subjected to a variety of different influences and without the correct unconditional space nature offers it will fail to see its true potential.

At a point in your personal healing when you've experienced a few awakenings you'll be open to listening to the lessons of wisdom while leaving the door open for all other elements. This is an in-between space of spiritual growth as you're trying to put the pieces together of your personal steps towards empowerment. People detect unusual or distant energies and anything outside of their scope will instantly trigger a reactive opinion and force a shutdown, as signs of positivity disturbs their environment's reality. A characteristic of a closed mind is that it aims to attack when they don't understand the circumstances. Energies that do not synchronise to their reality of hurt are classified as change and any sort of change that doesn't remotely link to the source of their pain is viewed from a fear-based belief, contained by the darkness that doesn't accept anything outside of their borders.

When a seedling has germinated and embraced its natural environment it grows with the idea of freedom, a pathway that is divinely guided. The interchangeable connection of energies is always realigning their value during every stage of internal and external growth. It acknowledges and accepts the transformation of growth and is supported by the collective enlightenment. A journey that can easily be mistaken by dismissing its growth as simple, looking from the outside in and placing subjective experiences on how you interpret the visual aspects of growth, is limited by the reflection of your eyes. The planet embraces the full embodiment of freedom, and it allows the transfer of energies to support the natural flow found in nature. The seedling still needs to provide acute attention to its surroundings, the freedom of life, supported by the circle of life. A network of energies that consciously acts as one but identifies the individual. Preliminary stages of growth dedicate large amounts of energy that try to understand the flow in which the circle of life is constantly adapting to stabilise its life force.

When you've entered a stage that acknowledges the value of an open mind, you're available to appreciate the individual's character that crosses your path. Being open to learning can and will attract unpleasant and unnecessary conditioning from others, but this isn't the first time in your life that you've experienced the ability to be open. When a newborn child is born, they are completely open to all elements. What you say and do to them, is taken as the truth. An energetic imprint of your teachings is absorbed within their reality, and even the smallest of addictions or personal habits are transferred across.

Stages of spiritual transformation are about listening to the footsteps of your journey that you have undertaken within this lifetime. The theme of enlightenment is about healing and heading towards inner peace. The tree of life holds the knowledge for those who are ready to listen. They build up an expansive principle of sending gratitude to all lessons learnt and experienced. Your healing and your attitude, is about that moment of sitting in the dark to welcome the light. As life goes on you will start to welcome new blessings of aligning sources. The tree of life first learns to be present in the changing environmental stabilising traits of nature but only really starts to connect when it recognises the aura which opens the senses of sensitivity to receiving energies.

Everyone's circumstances will always be different, and there is a chance that at some stage you will experience or be witness to a hostile atmosphere, and you will then be faced with the reality of how it affects you. The energies of an outburst will be aimed at everyone who is directly and indirectly present to the conditions of the outburst. A person that doesn't recognise energies, may detect the manner of the negativity that was conflictual, but with the tree of life it builds an aura, the bark that provides the ability to exist. For a person who has removed themselves from accepting the energies that run through them, they will always be subjected to external conflicts of passive aggressive energies. As you start laying the foundations of a peaceful mind and move with the wind trying to adapt with the natural changes of your embodiment, you'll soon build a field of awareness. Your open attitude to learning the transfer of energies slowly builds an intuitive detection system that supports the alignment of your values.

Detecting energies can and will be very draining. You've suddenly activated a realisation of your personal movements and how you attach your thoughts and actions to your beliefs. The processing of those default behaviours will come with a resistant energy of avoidance, so you dedicate enormous amounts of energy to try and relieve the burden. It is essential that you participate in your own life, supported by environments that allow you to heal. One of the first steps is embracing self-care by finding an outlet to ground and release all unwelcome energies that are the remains of someone else's storm. A process that helps remove the conflictual energies within your embodiment is a routine of honour. The attachment and removal are important, but it is merely the beginning to what qualities an aura will bring to your life.

Processing reactions, events and breaking down all parts of the transferred energy is an instinct of an aligned embodiment, but during times of healing, you will have to honour a step-by-step evaluation of your own actions compared to others. If you put yourself in a situation where you were potentially charging your emotional state to react, transferred energy from the past experiences could still hold a controlled pattern by charging your reaction. When reviewing energies, there is a process of healing where we look to the source. It is the source that holds the power and if you look around society, you will never see the true source of the narrative as it has healing qualities that can release people from their burden.

Healing is about letting go of the negative energies that have attached themselves to you and by identifying the source of the energy you can accept the release of that burden.

Typically, throughout any interaction, top down, they will drip feed you a version of the truth, as if you were to identify the source of the full truth, you would most likely disagree with their agenda. To obtain the status of control they are selective in their actions and the information in which they feed you. This narrative disempowers an individual's ability to process events as they occur.

CHAPTER 4

BALANCE

Balancing your mind to synchronise with the workings of your body can be a difficult reality when we reflect on how the operations of society are functioning. One of the first lessons that you seek to understand is the available space between you and other people. The foundation of your learning is by registering the actions of others. A transition that creates spaces for individuals to express the strength of their inner peace. Reflecting on your life and reviewing what spaces were available to you, will highlight areas that did not involve another person's opinion or ideologies that supported the benefits of the materialistic world. A balanced mind, body and soul requires personal space, supported by an unconditional environment that allows them to look from within, opening doors to listening and connecting to the answers that resonate within the aura of a divine light, a light that shines bright inside of you.

As you enter stages of healing, you may find yourself back tracking and searching for answers relating to the methods of the ideologies that were taught to you. Keeping in mind that healing is about seeing the blessings, so to form an opinion of blame is to move away from healing. Aiming to understand people's situations and how they were imbalanced due to teachings of others can open a mind that helps see the truth for what it stands for. A realisation that will assist you in letting go of all those uncomfortable moments, while welcoming energies that align to the balancing of your embodiment.

Most people who live in a materialistic world, would have missed the teaching of understanding a space that acknowledges the identity of a soul and its embodiment. You're looking to welcome a calm and aligned space into your aura. An ideology that may go against your current structure of how you operate. A condition where you actively fill your day to be as efficient as possible, but as peace crosses the horizon and the balancing of your mind will bring about the task of allowing the winds of change to welcome a place of harmony. It is not a device, or any knowledge that survives in a logical format that will highlight the path. Surrounding yourself with energies that reflect the balancing principles of nature will provide an opportunity to look at your life from within, a sacred place where it is only you that has the honour of viewing the unique purpose that balances your mind, body, and soul.

Our terminology and rules dictate the terms of how our language restricts the ability to spend time working on your mental health, and it is mental health that helps you balance your mind, body, and soul. The concept of equality is misleading and draws on you to disconnect from any form of healing if you're trying to work towards rebalancing your embodiment. Our point of reference is the qualities of the planet and the universe, we look to them when searching for our place and purpose. Within nature, and across the universe, there is not one energy that is equal, everything is uniquely balanced. It is a term that if you believe you are equal to others you do not register or accept the divine qualities of an individual's identity.

Equality disempowers your ability to think for yourself, so when you look at a person, you are left with the false narrative of categorising them. You will fail to notice the respect of the interaction as there is no other person or energy just like them. The balanced energies of your embodiment are forms of the unique combination that is displayed through different characters of nature. Masculine and Feminine energies that support the temple of one's physical purification. The connection of your embodiment to the energies of the universe synchronise with the balancing requires that it is forever adapting and changing, a divine language that opens the doors to wisdom beyond what a logical mind cannot see. Equality, or defining a group as equal, we place our predetermined formatted calculations, resulting in categorising the definition, a terminology which if we look towards the origin of the source, history will show us the era of slavery. To claim equality is to place yourself in the system of slavery.

The system sees you as a number, but you're much more than that and as we grow, our awareness of the energies is important. If we fail to adapt to the surroundings and get stuck in a repetitive pattern of someone else's reality, we gradually move away from the meaning of life. The balancing of your internal and external qualities can lead to a sharp realisation of how much you're repressing and rejecting your embodiment while numbing your reality, in order to fit into the model of society. While you are working on balancing your ability to be comfortable and relaxed within your mind, it's extremely easy to ignore the other parts that complete your embodiment. The abundant displays of how balancing occurs in nature, shows us that as we adapt, we recognise the whole of us. It is a transition that sees you for all the energies that complete you.

The importance of an expressive outlet that shows your creativity can unite your whole acknowledgement of your embodiment. While you are trying to work through stages of balancing your mind, body, and soul, it is a sign of expression that signals to the surrounding energies that you are willing to listen. The communication of the interchangeable, forever evolving energies of your existence is registered through your aura. An aura holds qualities and strength of an internal light. It can act as a deterrent for unwelcome energies while also detecting other energies that resonate with your internal frequencies. An empowerment that embraces a divine line of communication that is linked to alternative sources. Strengthening the balancing of your embodiment realigns your consciousness to attract lines of communication that you wouldn't normally be open to, just as the tree of life grows and adapts to the surrounding energies, the lines of communication that protect the internal blessings of life are all present through its outer skin.

During the initial stages of balancing your embodiment must be practical and relatable to your lifestyle, otherwise someone subjected to change can create a highly resistive attitude, displaying certain qualities that are highlighted by personal traits, such as anxiety, stress, fear, control, envy, and jealousy. All struggling to allow a place of self-awareness due to past traumas that have confined your approach to adapt. They are also symptoms of a mindset that is disconnected with no ability to regain power and composure. A reality where a lost mind will typically revert to a harsh and conflicted default stance that is aimed to sabotage their growth and stay within their borders of their mental safe zone. No matter what stage of the healing you are at it will take time, kindness, and a caring loving attitude with patience. To be strict and forceful, pushing away emotions and shutting down instincts is a concept of your teachings that have conditioned your behaviour. Trying to balance a part of you that has lost touch with your purpose is the reason it is important to have creative outlets that provide individualised expressions of yourself. Expressions that have been dormant inside of you, waiting to be called upon, and during this time of re-establishing and forming a connection it is important to have several different types of creative outlets that resonate with your embodiment. This allows your soul to blossom in times when a space of freedom is in balance.

Nature has this creative beauty of how it rebalances any condition that is thrown its way, allowing a growth of wisdom that manages to blossom in any terrain and climate. The seasons demonstrate the purification of adjusting and aligning yourself to rebalancing your relationship when searching for a point of reference. Just look at the seasons, a natural occurring event that no matter how bad one season is, it fails to impact the basic principle of a balanced universe. Natural disasters occur when an energy has created an imbalance and it is nature's way of removing certain energies to stabilise itself. A constant evolutionary flow of energy that is transferred to stabilise the divine source of the universe. Evolution will always transfer energy to be aligned with a pivotal point of balance, but as humans we project and transfer a lot of anger, stress, and anxiety out into the world, an expression of pain that is now gaining momentum, momentum that the earth and universe will seek to correct. Our current mindset dictates that because we have lost touch with the meaning of life and all we end up doing is fighting ourselves, ignoring the lessons of nature and not appreciating the beauty that is available.

The trajectory of the planet is always changing, adapting but constantly reverting to a point of balance. An energy that stabilises and produces long term foresights, a simple reflection of how your life within this time should be. The amount of time that you dedicate to yourself will reflect on the space you hold and the ability to recognise the harmonic frequencies that are present, an enlightenment that can set a long-term foundational core principle for years and generations to come. A cycle of wholeness that is balanced because you committed to yourself and allowed supportive energies that create an enormous amount of positive momentum moving forward. Balancing your empowerment, your purpose, and your ability to adapt and change is a lifetime commitment to a higher consciousness.

Throughout all days and in all moments, we can open and close spaces. Energetic zones that will either protect and empower us or allow the energy to be transferred unknowingly, freely giving away your empowerment. Our daily routines and habits will be different for everyone. However, they can easily be broken down into spaces and when you concentrate on one space that also can be divided across several different influencing energies. The pathway we take to understanding ourselves requires an acknowledgement of our actions, feelings, and thoughts and by identifying all segments and aspects of our lives we can then start to reflect on certain energies.

The willingness to transfer energies due to lack of control is the point of imbalance. Not knowing yourself and the true alignment can force a complex integration of controlling energies to merge into a cloud that does not clear. Imbalances such as personal time, work, socialising, exercising all merging and creating confusion, only to allow people to influence and control your opinions and actions. By committing to understanding the core principles of open and closing spaces it empowers you and allows a balanced lifestyle, protecting from unwelcome and controlling elements. Understanding the merging of energies is important.

A lot of ambitious people dedicate their lives to a cause that they become passionate about, a drive that can easily confuse the lines between personal and professional. Being enthusiastic and committed to a cause is not necessarily a bad thing and could very well be a principle that it may be part of your soul's contract, but modern-day society does not have any boundaries. For many companies, physical and mental health will never come before profits and ambitions. You are a cog in their wheel that can always be replaced. A simple concept that is common across all aspects of every community, it doesn't matter what job you hold, what your position in life is or even if you have a family or not. The world's industries success is on the back of your mental health, so identifying spaces allows boundaries and protects you from all periods of overreach from friends, work, technology etc. Holding a space does not just enlighten your journey but allows an awareness of other people's spaces and boundaries, showing them respect and treating them as an individual soul.

Opening and closing spaces has so many basic qualities it is quite easy to implement values of self-awareness, values that allow you the honour of being in the moment. A period that helps identify your actions and your daily routines, while acknowledging and understanding other people's lives. It is also one of the first steps to internal empowerment with the result of raising your vibration to a level that will resonate with your higher self. The initial transition when first acknowledging and evaluating key areas of your life will concentrate on how honest and in touch you are with internal peace.

Distancing yourself from external influences allows you a period of time that expands your attention to an honest and true reflection on which conditionings deliberately restrict your progress and disregards your personal space. Over any stage of growth and enlightenment, you'll be constantly readjusting your stance, realigning your ideology and repositioning your identity. A place of disconnection surrounded by pain, fear and stress is a slow and delicate journey. By allocating the space to understand the healing process shows how much control you truly have in your life.

Spaces are about being in the moment, bringing your self-awareness to habits, ideologies, routines, and energies while managing and identifying all external influences. A critical first step and example of space is your sleep. The sleeping habits and patterns you create will reflect on how beneficial that personal space is for you. Sleep is influenced by every event, emotions, and feelings that you are subjected to during the days, weeks, and months. Small, unhealthy, and unnatural daily addictions control the status of your mind, pushing and restricting simple basic harmonic frequencies out of balance to compromise a deeper connection. Items like mobile phones, TV shows, the news, social media, work, friends, and social life all affect your sleep. All these external energies just end up draining your ability to reflect and rebalance your physical and mental state.

Outlining the space for your health and wellbeing, is a period that you dedicate to yourself for rest, rejuvenation, and reflection. The idea of sleep always starts in your mind when you're ready to allocate a space. It's important to identify the space prior to sleep, removing all objects that have attached to your foresight while dedicating a supportive routine that cleanses and removes all energies. All spaces require accountability and responsibility on your part. The basic concept is easy, but it comes down to your own standards, and how much you're willing to become the best part of yourself. This will be challenged by addictions like eating habits, technology, ideologies, and conditioning that will all stand in your way, and they will continue to prevent you from healing because you try to revert to your default state.

Placing yourself in an environment that concentrates on you is foreign to us and a reality that may take a little adjustment to get used to. The average lifestyle must seek excuses and reasons why not to participate in your own existence. Having an unhealthy routine during any stage of your day can and will affect your sleep, it will always be compromised if your defaulting patterning persists on neglecting areas like diet and exercise routine. Pushing boundaries with opinions and conditioned beliefs are all signs of rejecting the balancing principles of your embodiment. With this lifetime it is one of the greatest journeys of honour to participate in the health and wellbeing of our mind, body, and soul.

The acknowledgment of spaces will help support and respect other spaces, knowing that inside of you is a conscious power that can trigger the processes of self-awareness, when reviewing the relationships of your environment. Empowerment involves being present when you consciously know that you're opening and simultaneously closing a space. The relationship towards any space where you are naturally jumping from one open space to the next, it's an important aspect to self-awareness, especially when identifying your daily habits, to stamp or acknowledge the transition as you close one, you're directly opening another. Sleep is a good starting point. Not only can you remove your daily environmental workings, but you are opening the space to place in a moment of self-care and by creating a healthy routine where you can allocate your attention to a healthy line of communication, you're sending a welcome message that you're ready to listen.

To start off with, by recognising your actions can actively draw a closure to a space. It's practical to add a symbol, phrase, or an action as you build a healthy relationship with your mind, a simple message of acknowledgment. When you head to bed to sleep, it could be as simple as you open the space by brushing your teeth and looking in the mirror, then when you look to close the space after a period of sleep you may choose to make your bed. Simple routines that you already do, but you've adding the value of acknowledging the energies and importance of self-care.

Balancing spaces isn't just about the idea of opening and closing different energetic windows within the moment, it helps reflect on all energies that have crossed paths with your personal journey. There will be a point in time where you can use it as a reference in re-establishing your aligning values. Areas of life that affect the change of your personalities will have an influence on how you react to the environment when faced upon alternative motives and social agendas. A wave of energy that can affect your ideologies, addictions, and philosophical restrictions. These can all become a critical point that is pushed by the wave that forces a mindset of denial and refusal of the idea that part of your life has been formed and structured on the teachings that have separated you from your identity, an area that reflects on the responsibility you hold to accepting that a part of your character has been fuelled by a conditioned reality. Opening and closing spaces are integrated by multiple different layers of self-awareness and accountability. The events of the day still need to be reviewed and processed to correctly interpret and accept the experiences, for an internal processing of these events.

During reflection, a strong intuition allows a deeper connection to your aura and will relay messages to and from the subconscious mind that you may have missed. This will allow you to pick up and evaluate all energies that have been directed and crossed over into your aura.

Big energetic and dominant moments can become overwhelming and easily spread across all areas of your day, pushing boundaries between all personal and professional spaces, and by allocating dedicated times to purely reflect on the events within the moment allows you to access a deeper understanding of being able to review the energies that were unable to be processed earlier on in the day.

When reviewing a space there can be two similar circumstances but they hold different energies that are supported by different underlining messages. Breaking down the spaces helps understand the balance of your aura and how to attach or detach the relevant energy, knowing that a procedure of self-awareness highlights your intentions of aligning a space of respect to a higher consciousness of being present. There will also be spaces where you've committed a personality to the surroundings, a personality that holds certain protective boundaries, allowing you to attract only the energies and messages that are aligned to your own individualised journey. Identifying spaces is one of the first steps towards your enlightenment and your wellbeing, but as you evolve you will realise that there will be times within those spaces that you will be required to step out of and acknowledge that you have moved into a new space with new energies and new vibrational alignments. Every area and space that you are subjected to will be a test of your mental and physical wellbeing. It's how you choose to process the wisdom and learn the lessons that are on hand, an important lesson when reflecting on how balanced your actions and thoughts are.

As you move towards aligning your values and start to recognise spaces that complete your daily routines, it may bring your awareness to certain spaces that you've been subjected to that have shaped the scene with a constant overreach and disempowerment of boundaries. The shift in which the energies change should never be about avoidance, but now it's in your empowerment to create and form these boundaries. Supported by the network of being polite, graceful, holding respect but not accepting the overreach. Afterall, no one is entitled to attack someone's self-care and mental health. Self-awareness will be a journey where you didn't realise how much energy you were freely giving away, discharging your ability to align with an internal peace.

When balancing your life, you will seek to reflect on every aspect of your character, looking upon instrumental life changing events of the past and present, while recognising the correlation of how they drive future events. Situations where you have dedicated large amounts of energy to places that hold a significant emotional influence over your actions and thoughts. The topic of personal responsibility may dominate the reaction of change, healing, and peace as it is a slow journey, you adapt with the winds of change as you are constantly realigning your values to a place of harmony when experiencing a moment of enlightenment. Much of our lives can represent the dedication to education and work, substantial amounts of time working towards a lifestyle that is accepted and recognised for the collective benefits of society. Our mental and physical states of health are determined under a set of parameters that supports the benefits of a blanket reality. Your daily avoidance restricts the relevance of how you process your mental reality. Its designed process of repeating a repetitive schedule can easily create a theme that runs on autopilot.

The initial breakdown of your direct routine will be critical to how you interpret the space that you experience throughout a standard day. Work is a dominant force that influences our mindset, it can dominate the conversation and easily spill over and affect everything that is involved when working towards your mental and physical health. Defining the lines could be difficult in how your mind understands the boundaries, blurring a reality that directly affects your state of balance. Our practical daily routines have areas of diet, exercise, periods of self-care, socialising, and work, these all contribute to the workings that can balance and support your health or can function as a deterrent to avoid personal responsibility for the identity of your health.

Spaces are essential to balancing your lifestyle and supporting others to create a community that accepts and understands the available information that has been missed when an overreach has blurred the lines of personal boundaries. The routine in which you get to work will all be specific to the type of job and the type of work you undertake but for most you leave your home in the morning and head to a site, or an office, or even on the road. As you reflect the breakdown of your routine, you will find an image of when you mentally place yourself within the energy of work, a task where many people would say as they are leaving the house, they mention they're heading to work. A statement that draws your attention to a window of entering a state of work.

During your day, as you become efficient with achieving goals, the mind allows the activities for exercise, or a casual catch up with friends for a drink, or even food shopping to save time later. Without defining the spaces of your routines, they will all contribute to the umbrella of work. Areas of your life that serve in balancing your embodiment and the attention required towards self-care and respect now contribute all your energy to a period of work that disempowers your identity, it removes the spaces that assist in the balancing of the mental and physical relationship of your personal empowerment.

As work overflows into your personal life, the parameter in which you value in a family environment can soon reflect the traits in which you operate at work. To be as efficient as possible, an efficiency to avoid, does not allow a space that offers close friends and family a caring loving quality and acknowledging the space of peace as it works outside the logical profile of efficiency. It's about seeing the blessings that are present in a moment of love. The balancing of your identity and self-care, should always recognise the respect for others and the essential principles of a home.

CHAPTER 5

RELATIONSHIP WITH NATURE

A place that is lost, a paradise that offers us freedom, but as we look in the mirror, we are unable to identify any part of us that belongs. As a lost soul, unfound and unidentified, as their relationship with nature is in denial, as their attitude is to continue with the emotional theme of building houses. A default patterning of shaping a limited mindset that serves the greed of a conditioned reality. A mindset that indicates our superior presence on this planet while justifying our ignorance, only to proclaim that we are the most advanced lifeforce and species. A statement that confirms the ego of a troubled mind, to declare such passive aggressive ideologies removes the values of being present to abundant qualities of what nature can provide. An advanced culture or species knows the value of peace, and the qualities of respect across all energies, while upholding the core principles of what completes the universe. It doesn't seek to destroy, but to acknowledge the harmonic balances of being able to appreciate this honour of living life through a divine experience.

The lessons of accountability that are present are repressed when we reflect on our historical actions and directions, highlighting the arrogance of our control that does not recognise the importance of peace. Our language dictates the theme of our repetitive behaviour that constantly repeats the same patterning of standards. The greed of the economy deliberately avoids the lessons that should be learnt from the previous generations, as it creates a loop of denial, a transfer of energy that doesn't synchronise to the high vibrational qualities of the planet. Refusing accountability and ignoring the essential part of our growth, they attach the theme of an emotionally charged system that just repeats the same looping patterns. From generation to generation, a wave of rejecting all natural properties of the planet, unaware of the sacred teachings of an advanced society that knows the magic of being open to listening to its environment. Thousands of years that have been built on a disconnected reality of acknowledging people's souls, rejecting their purpose when walking along the fertile plains of mother nature.

A divine language is the energy that completes you, a network linked to your time and the internal status of your navigation, the transfer of energy that provides singular alignment across all organic systematic clocks, providing a space that ticks to a higher vibrational internal guidance system.

The meaning of a home is understanding that nature provides an in-house experience of self-identification. An unconditional space that mixes the tranquillity of internal peace and freedom, to the harsh reality of the circle of life.

Two interactions that can both stop and start the heart within a moment, an unconditional place that sees life and knows how to balance the planet. Our internal navigation system is a network that is linked to the unseen workings of nature. Our embodiment should reflect the core principles as a direct example of how to honour the circle of life. Within your body there will be energies from past lives supported by a variety of different experiences, all adding to the knowledge of being part of the collective consciousness. The transfer of energy is the history of previous lifeforms and consciousness that have all experienced different energetic qualities, the collective supports the expansive blessings as we look towards the meaning of life.

One topic that is sensitive across different opinions is our diet. We don't look to the balancing principle of life, but we choose to lead with selfish narratives. A narrative that doesn't recognise the transfer of energy that supports the circle of life. The organic nature in which you absorb the knowledge and quality of the food you eat; is how you recognise the divine values that complete the transfer of the energy in your embodiment. If we look towards the life of a chicken and what type of variety of lifestyle it is subjected to, we can soon start to understand. A chicken that is locked up, does not have any available access to natural forms of exercise and has little or no access to sunlight. It is subjected to a high protein diet as the agenda is to maximise profit, which depends on the weight of the chicken. They are also restricted on socialising, communication with other organic species within nature and experience a limited timeframe. Whereas a chicken, who lives an organic life, exercises in a natural environment, supported by an organic natural diet, socialising, and communicating across all types of animals. Two quite separate ways of breeding chickens, but as you look towards the circle of life, what you eat is the transfer of what type of energy the chickens' lives are subjected to. Traits that can either restrict your natural ability to be healthy or transfer the complete balance of the circle of life through you. Our gratitude is the appreciation of having the honour of being privileged to the unique qualities of what you eat. The gratitude for freedom.

The same principles apply to fruit and vegetables. Natural sunlight and organic fertilisers supported by other elements during its growth, as it absorbs the energetic transfers. A supportive network of organic products. If we move towards a chemical lifestyle of products, we look towards the origins of the existence and the intent of its evolution, most pesticides and chemically restrictive products are a sub-product of a war. Change and adapted to control the growth of your food, a product that was invented to kill or create pain and anger isn't a product that is welcomed into the circle of life. What you welcome into your diet is a reference point of how much you respect nature. The transfer of energy into our diets create a unique embodiment that can represent certain qualities and traits. Allowing the transfer of experiences can represent anything from a fish in a river, to a goat on the highest mountain, or even a bee that sees the world from a different point of view.

Our internal compass that resonates to the navigation system of the planet is about understanding the divine principles when recognising the type of influential energies that participate in your lifestyle. Then you start to create a picture of how they resonate with the circle of life. The internal compass resonates to different vibrational frequencies across all parts of the planet. Every place has its own unique set of balancing conditions, an environment that requires time and a caring loving attitude of appreciation towards its vibrational principles. When we observe our diet and referencing the surrounding balancing attributes of nature, our internal compass must synchronise to the values in which energies are relevant during that space, a critical part when we look to find our way with the circle of life.

The frequencies of the environment grow and adapt to the source of the energy in that place. We currently treat the world as one, a simple system where we control and dictate every market. A mindset that doesn't understand the unique environmental characteristics of individual places. The wisdom of allowing your internal navigation system to recognise the individualised characters of the selected place takes time, potentially years to listen and recognise what's required in matching the balancing frequencies. Our lack of knowledge and an attitude that seeks to conquer only to profiteer creates a trajectory that will only ever destroy whatever stands in our way. As you walk through nature, you're not looking back to see the damage of your footsteps, but to know that every moment forward is aligned with the silhouette of nature.

The deepest form of healing you can experience is looking and recognising the person you see in the mirror, a journey that needs to be supported by the collective consciousness of our universe. Allowing a space of true freedom is understanding the past experiences and ideologies in how you see the world. You can never truly understand yourself if you don't start to recognise the characteristics of how your alignment matches with the high vibrational frequencies that complete the planet. When you look to nature, you must see yourself, but a lost soul can't see habits and ideologies that are suppressing their vision of how the world truly exists. Your mind isn't about the restrictions of being placed within the picture frame, but the freedom of accepting that you are part of a collective space.

The teachings of listening to what knowledge is available is by learning the principles of honour, it will open new avenues that align with the planet. Our current state of projection is targeted towards a lifestyle that we are fixated on our own pain, the furthest away from a collective reality that we can be. There is knowledge that can be accessed by activating your whole embodiment and the information of a divine connection that is available when you move away from the logical programmed conditions. The way we see energy in the moment fulfils a narrative that is unnatural to the planet. Our connection on how we harness energy is placed upon our internal understandings of core principles. To understand the energies that complete you, is a history of diverse types of experiences, life forms that have understood and been part of the divine language of nature.

The transfer of energy of all the food you eat can allow those experiences to enlighten your journey.

Nature creates a space for an advanced network to navigate across all dimensions, a force that is also linked to our internal compass when reviewing our place of navigation. One of the most supportive lifeforces we have available if we are willing to allow ourselves the privilege of being open to receiving messages that align with our own accountability. The direct link to the fourth dimension is a network of energy that assists you when moving towards a place where peace comes from within. It is the dimension that can physically assist you on this journey. Spirits from past or present lives, are all waiting to try and help you when an available opportunity arises.

Every time you are contemplating life struggles or searching for an answer to a problem, within your world, through every room you walk into, or every valley to look down, there is energy that supports your journey. The energies are there to help and assist you, but as always it depends on how much empowerment and freedom is available for you to think for yourself.

Our mindset will be drawn to the open space of avoidance, and as people move towards a spiritual path, they will experience different stages of awakening. Some may link their space to a dimension outside of the place you call home, an additional source of wisdom that's available beyond the planet. It can also be an area that can force a spiritual ego to avoid the accountability of your mind, body, and soul. Disregarding the deepest forms of healing, is a foresight where you can actively try and forget about the past. Life on this planet is about embracing your physical form, healing at the deepest level is always hard and emotional but aligns with a direction of the purest appreciation when we acknowledge ourselves. Your internal navigation of physical reality is divinely linked across knowing yourself and understanding the cycle of life, by seeing your purpose as a reflection in nature.

The relationship with yourself and recognizing your internal compass is aligned and linked directly through your aura. Seeing the silhouette of your empowerment attracts energies that allow you to activate parts of your mind that have been placed upon restrictions or forced into deep hibernation. The internal navigation that connects you to the stars, the planets and other dimensions is through a conduit that leads to the foundation of core principles. It opens your eyes as it connects in with a vibrational map of the planet, allowing you to see the purest form of enlightenment. It is what your third eye sees as home.

We restrict our lines of communication, typically defaulting to our verbal expression. The nature in the way we have created our languages through communication was to survive, it is a secondary intuition in which we must learn. We are born with a divine language that connects in with the blessings of life, searches the network as you navigate your vision of enlightenment towards all relevant lessons of life. There are many types of branches that communicate across the different layers of self-awareness and gratitude. We are connected to our spirits that are trying to communicate and positively support our journey by sending an array of messages, an energy that typically comes directly from the fourth dimension.

The world within a world where only your third eye has the honour of seeing the whole picture. Our relationship with nature holds certain values, it represents characters and personalities that reflect the energy of individuals as you seek to identify the workings of the planet. Our direct lines of communication will hold meaning of importance towards individuals that have blessed our lives. During their life they present a special meaning to the volume of how they influence you and your relationship with them, but after and as soon as they become one with nature, they quickly represent the elements of a divine energy of a balanced system. Sending messages of guidance and protection as they travel, flowing through the wind while you continue to walk along the journey of life.

When we look towards the fourth dimension it is our direction of internal guidance that leads us towards the door. The unseen is freedom beyond the physical restrictions, it has layers of meanings that is internally linking our connection towards nature, the cosmos, and our close relationships. The balancing elements of the planet are linked through us and throughout the universe. When we move towards a period of self-care and self-love, we look to find our true embodiment, not guided by motives or agenda but a place of freedom. The balancing elements that we require to identify harmony within ourselves will eventually become apparent that we have always had the privilege of being witness to the unique vibrational network of nature, opening a consciousness that sees what energies run through you and to the collective network that stabilises the universe.

The breakdown of how you start to see the world understands the teachings of certain aspects that the planet represents. The relationship within our lifetime creates instrumental places of harmony that hold personal memories. Memories that you are here to experience. Opening your reality and looking at life through all elements will assist in transforming your journey. Being present to life moments that represent a special person will hold a connection to certain elements as that bond moves towards creating memories that are close to your heart. The influential individual that is linked to those memories will walk into nature and their silhouette will mimic the divine connection to a particular place that is part of a balanced world. A soul carries on supporting you in the fourth dimension after their time is up if your relationship was built on a foundation of pure kindness and respect. They will stay and support you until it's your time to let them go. You will evolve and adapt as you continue experiencing the moments of life. There is always that one point, a milestone where internal places of freedom acknowledge your appreciation, as you know the time is right for them to move on.

The loyalty and kindness that secures the foundations of your family are linked to a special line of communication as we look towards the divine teachings of nature. We know that our whole embodiment is made up from memories that cover a variety of different sources. Our DNA, the transfer of the energetic stamps that are unique to our diet and the environmental traits of our place that we call home are just a few of the energies that are linked across our life experiences. It is a network that works together, collectively synchronising a higher knowing of what love can bring into someone's life. Older generations of families have had a direct influence over all generations that followed, as they embrace their path and move towards fulfilling their life's purpose. They know that within nature is a familiar face that looks on no matter what stage of life is present. It is the energy that sparks the enlightenment of freedom when opening a space of being able to look into nature and seeing loved ones display their personality.

The souls that move on and become another part of the collective consciousness are not only here for guidance and support, it's about honour and celebration, remembering our gratitude and love. The value of being in the moment and part of the collective network that respects the space of gatherings that honour the meaning of life. Knowing that special occasions from select dates to ceremonies are themes of respect, as you acknowledge that it is not all about what you have in the physical form, but those who are still present in the collective. Welcoming all spirits and guides to an unconditional space that acknowledges their presence, an energy that is built on the foundations of peace and love.

Our internal guidance system can look to nature for navigation through tough and questionable times. The divine language of our core principles knows that your journey isn't about walking it alone but to use the elements and the support of spirits to see the light. We can link our internal compass to the stars, natural elements, and qualities of the global compass. Attaching spirits to select elements will welcome energies to life lessons that can highlight your path, for a family that looks forward knows that whatever came before them is looking down with guidance. The transfer of energy in the fourth dimension isn't just directly related to family, it covers every pattern that is provided by animals and spirits that join us throughout key moments of our life, moments that are destined to support our awakenings. There are spirits that won't leave your side until the time has arrived, and then there are some that come and go as they like to drop in for a chat.

Every creature that crosses your path has a meaning and it holds wisdom of the greater understanding. Our visual display of avoiding accountability confirms that we do not hold any kind of respect when driving our agendas. We push the world to an imbalance that affects all environments and now the planet is constantly trying to realign the energies. Our desire to kill or remove has triggered a divine reaction of karma, history and actions that have had devastating effects on the planet and all life forces. It is never anyone's right to kill and eliminate for fun. This is an attitude of denial that reiterates we are lost and that we have always been lost. There have been many eras of human races prior to this one, an advanced society that does not leave unnecessary devastating effects across the planet, our footprint that only understands the pain and anger fuelling our continuous arrogant stance of a destructive mindset. We seek power at the expense of anything that stands in its way, heading in the complete opposite direction to our true purpose of this lifetime.

A general lifestyle will indicate that nature to them is extremely limited and see it as tasks of garden maintenance like mowing or trimming the hedge, while making a point of taking a picture. A picture does not tell the story of an individual. For most that do take pictures it is for the reason of trying to search for their soul. The memories that you entail are part of you, and during stages of your life, some memories are so important that it's necessary to record their value. It is when you use pictures for the purpose of avoiding the moment that shows the internal struggles of how you understand your value within this lifetime. To hold a restrictive ideology of how it influences you in the future will stop any natural flow of abundance that accepts your identity and the true beauty of being in the moment. We create distractions and move our attention away from seeing the truth of what's presented to us. Our addictions and routines of avoidance will always hinder your ability to see outside of the picture frame. The picture you seek isn't just by looking with your eyes.

Hobbies and ideologies can be methods of looking to express what we see within our mind, an outlet to stop the storm from circulating. When we investigate nature, we are always privileged to see natural displays of creative outlets. Our language sometimes cannot describe how you feel, but our conditioned reality has set the terms that we believe our expression is through verbal attention. The constant motive for reassurance that drives a calling that success must be achieved and is attributed to the amount of attention we receive. A successful life is different for everyone, our souls contract knows the direction in which we should look to follow.

For peace and accepting our embodiment we must look towards committing to our lives, a soul needs to unite its attention and allow an expression of self-care as it seeks to recognise a free mind. Creative outlets are all about self-healing, feeling at peace and building on the relationship of our whole embodiment and as we turn our attention to nature, we can witness a variety of different creative outlets that are in plain sight.

Nature's ability to rejuvenate and balance the world is by having the available collective space of grounding, it holds you in a place that energises the flow that helps remove the unwelcome and controlling reality mindsets. Any stage of early healing sees nature as a distant reality, a mindset that finds it hard to see why people call it home. As a society we create concrete jungles that are supported by chemically bound products of destruction, instantly stopping any natural availability to ground. Our reality is only then limited to the compounds that contain our mind, it doesn't offer any alternative way of releasing pain or separating spaces. This is a highly concentrated reality that targets your inability to self-identity, leading to control and a negative environment. The freedom that nature offers can be for some, an internal struggle to understand their place within the world. Their mindset is built on the narrative of a materialistic control that dominates the functioning of society.

When we have the honour of holding a space that grounds and connects us into a universal consciousness and as it can open new doors that allow us to see the world differently. We look to recognise little personality traits that highlight the expressive value of a life. It can assist you in raising your vibrational alignment to a source that is completely engaged in the collective network of the universe. When you look to express yourself by reflecting on the inspirational environmental workings of a divine source, you don't look to become someone else, you look to welcome their energy and let it flow through you while creating an outlet that raises your vibrational consciousness.

Everywhere you look in nature there are lessons that can help as we look towards finding our own individualised expression, they adapt and change to the transfer of energy. As the element brushes through nature, you can easily find sources of inspiration. The wind that flows through the trees, it bends and releases, shifting and supporting the transfer of energy. Allowing the wind to highlight the value of an expressive outlet that supports all-natural ability to interact.

As you turn your attention to animals, a bird that flies effortlessly as it guides through the wind, or a dog shaking the water off its coat, or even a penguin that looks to balance its egg on its feet while keeping it warm. If you have a positive and open mind you will see that any animal and natural environment has their own unique expression and as it adapts to the embedded network of its identity, it is always supported with the balancing principles of the universe. Outlets like singing, dancing, painting, playing music and meditation are just some of the creative outlets that can assist your journey. An internal gratification knows that a creative outlet is an expression of freedom and all the answers you seek are already in plain sight.

CHAPTER 6

CORE PRINCIPLES

Core principles are unfamiliar territory for most humans. Our existence is built up on two different paths that have influenced the way we stand here today. We have a past that is driven by chaos, parts of our memory and attitude are based on conflicts and holds a savage historical patterning when we review our origins. We weren't much more than scavengers fighting for scraps of food, no order or loyalty, and the conditions were only the fittest survive. Every other creature on this planet has adapted and evolved to their own special characteristic of their species, a uniquely bound method on how they survive and naturally becomes part of the circle of life. Our trajectory is a little different to most, as we've evolved we have gained a little assistance from an advanced race along the way. The introduction of rules and how to start the growth of a society, only to be burdened by our origins. The purest form of our trajectory isn't about the constant expansion of emotionally charged population growth, but connecting into a system of enlightenment, accessing our true and full ability, the power of understanding the divine that is directly linked to our core principles.

Our minds are defaulted to the logical ingrained reality that has survived by chaos, a system that no matter what circumstance stands in our way, we constantly repeat the same patterns and problems. It is not that we can't evolve peacefully, but it's because we don't know anything different than control and death. Originally people would kill others to just eat a meal, and by introducing rules and regulations, instead of adapting to evolve peacefully, we changed the rules to suit our pain.

Our patterning behaviour is selfish, not because we don't have the capacity to be better but because we don't have gratitude and appreciation in our beliefs when looking upon our planet.

The way we operate hasn't changed; it is still the survival of the fittest. We still gamble, steal, kill and destroy, all bold words but if we step back and look how mankind has evolved, there is extraordinarily minor change in the way we carry out those methods. We fear anything different; we look to take what is not ours and then use our powers to control others.

The timelines are different, but the attitude is the same. There is a new change approaching on the horizon, a change that will look towards a new era as sections of society evolve into a peaceful state that recognises individualised embodiments. The era of accessing the true potential when looking towards your mental health, and the key is peace. Parts of society that look to control and destroy will always repeat their default patterning, but those who choose to connect in with nature and don't look to use those methods of control will move away from addictive states like technology, drugs, and alcohol, while acknowledging that a war is part of an ego that gives power to a group of people. This process will not happen overnight, and as you commit to your internal peace, the realisation that is supported by awakenings may enlighten a pathway of being the legacy for your family as you move forward. The origin of technology was always about evolving but we now have a choice in how we use it. It is part of the future, but for those who want to repeat their attitude of a restrictive ideology that is attached to their origins will only see it as a tool to seek power to destroy.

During this stage of evolution, we will always debate our purpose as we don't understand our identity. The reason for life will always be open to interpretation and depending on your values and experiences it will form a particular reality of how you see the world, influencing your opinions on whether our history will lead to a future of humble new beginnings. No matter what stage of your spiritual journey is enlightening you, it's the knowing of respect that will flow with your own evolution, moving towards a collective consciousness as we enter into a period of self-awareness. Activating an awakening that will slowly move through the planet, an energy that recognizes that we are about to enter a new stage. Our personal reaction will determine how we cope with learning lessons from past mistakes, a platform that will allow people to heal and the appreciation of understanding the value of being given this honour. The process of accountability is one of the first acknowledgements that you dedicate to yourself as you look to move towards a peaceful future.

Relationships are built on trust and love, and we create homes to share experiences. For most, it is also your fortress as you try to escape the harsh reality of our society. Our stance on behavioural patterns brings out the worst in people's attitude when they are faced or placed upon a survival mode when someone is targeted. Openly supported by greed or power, the instincts of our origins once again play a critical part in our beliefs, locking yourself away to survive an ideology that goes against the principles of life, as nature is all about the expansive consciousness that offers freedom.

Before we look at the spiritual realm of core principle our attention is brought to the appreciation for yourself. Basic life principles on how you operate is complicated, full of complex situations where your character will be challenged across all moments. Moments where one decision of yours can affect and change other people's lives across a variety of different outcomes. Our personal state of mind is the first step to addressing the type of standards and beliefs we hold. There is always a moment where a stagnant trail of reality has highlighted difficult and challenging situations. Times where critical but necessary decisions must be addressed. When our character is tested, the way we react controls the relationship of our own beliefs and principles. Do you allow people to explain their point of view, or is it easier to shut people down as we are not taught to understand people's emotions? It is easier to glide through life by staying outside the radar of accountability because in most situations it is only you that determines the value of how much respect you have for yourself. A common excuse used is that your actions towards others are in line with the rules and regulations of society. But to hold a truthful account of your actions, rules and regulations are designed to avoid them as they are not designed to honour a space so you can work on your mental health.

The feeling of being lost or missing a key part of your life, is connected to your relationship of understanding the strength of internal awareness and its foundations, which will determine how much of your life is controlled by your own decisions and how much of actions are controlled by another set of conditions. Time in your reality and any reality is never consistent. Your daily decisions are made on the grounds of what type of respect and underlining beliefs are part of you. When times are emotionally good, it's easy to remove yourself from the moment and revert to autopilot, easily forgetting simple life basics in a disconnected flow that once gained momentum can become uncontrollable, until it breaks down. A place of peace is a moment in control, releasing the urge to control others, a state of consciousness that identifies the ability to make decisions that doesn't project a lack of control in order to gain control. By being in control of yourself takes a place of reference to ground and reflect, a moment of silence that allows a greater perspective of your surroundings, a divine moment that flows with the harmonic frequencies of the planet. Being present and in the moment means you're on your own time, a reference that highlights a large part of life, aligning to a set of principles that don't take away your power, but enlightens a space of peace.

If your ideology is to shame and disrespect people, as you don't agree with their opinions, or project aggressive forms of hate, they are all symptoms of a disconnected reality with no identity. Every expression you have always comes from an internal source, it doesn't matter if it's your ideology or someone else's teachings of an ideology. To project opinions and to attack, means your verbal expressions have some truth when you look from within. As the hurricane circles, it is your reality that you're expressing. It is also a reality where you won't get the honour of moving towards a peaceful and respectful environment. To connect with core principles, you must be accountable for the energies that circulate around your mind. Breaking that barrier within the picture frame is accepting that within your mind you're allowed to be at peace. Feeling love and healing while floating towards the balancing principles of life.

Our present attention will be directly focused on the forces that are driving our actions. It is a highly volatile and emotional state, a space that requires the deepest of appreciation for self-accountability when reviewing our life, in a moment where forgiveness will be a topic that can clear a clouded reality. As our conditioning kicks in we revert to look at life through the default patterning of focusing our pain on a concentrated part of our vision. It is a reality that believes their pain is the truth, a power that when you lock yourself within the picture frame of a limited mind's capacity it stays disconnected within the parameters of your safe room. You only accept and limit your hearing to the voices that accompany you. When we look at core principles, if you're not willing to embrace your happiness you will stay locked up within the confined spaces of fear.

The constant attention to pain pushes values and principles outside the parameters of a peaceful reality and can very easily create a mob style reaction, a trait that is built into your system from thousands of years ago. No matter which area you choose to look at in society, through the cracks you will see the workings that are present in the underlining message of an emotionally charged survival instinct that is no better off than when the day rules were introduced to us. As we enter a new era, we will be moving away from disconnected realities and move towards an in-tune alignment that matches the vibrational principles of the planet.

We were given the opportunity to see the full picture when taught about rules and order, basic skills to allow communities to come together. Our natural instincts were too great of a hindrance for us to be able to acknowledge the lessons and see our true potential. Our survival fight or flight reaction was driven by our innate conscious behaviours that failed to recognise peace. Throughout history you can see wisdom where certain communities, religions or tribes have tried to teach or record the balancing principles of the planet. Opening the mind to a completely new world is hard for an instinct that is used to surviving by inflicting pain onto others.

As we enter this new era and just like the beginning, substantial amounts of the population will not gravitate towards understanding the basics of core principles. A foreseen reality that we should not try and change. Some people are born to teach, others to learn essential life skills and then young souls who are just at the start of their embodiment will use most of this life getting used to their experience. Remembering that divine timing is always an indicator that we are forever the eternal student. It takes lifetimes to go through all the lessons and teachings but as we approach a new beginning, we are setting the foundation of an advanced race that looks to give people the best opportunity upon entering this world. Young soul or old, a space of enlightenment will free the reality and realign our journey towards the core principles of life. Change will never happen overnight, and the lessons of freedom will take generations to truly understand the values of core principles, especially when learning the energies of the land you call home.

Core principles is the star above the tree of life, and it links every tree and journey to the divine source, it sees your value and your individualised identity. When we grow and evolve into our purpose, throughout every different stage of our embodiment we see the source divinely connected to a network that links all consciousness and principles together. Every part of the energetic transfer that is sent down from the divine source is received through a beam of light, a higher collective that supports the vibrational alignment, linking to all forms of communications across all sacred teachings. The light that shines down and attaches to every branch as your own embodiment harmonises is a new period of enlightenment, a test of character that only finds the answer through experiences and searching for the internal alignment. As a soul attaches to its embodiment, it will be faced with understanding its own identity, acknowledge the peace when reflecting on the health of their mind, body, and soul, and then sees the unconditional spaces that recognise the respectful boundaries to the knowledge of freedom. Three areas of growth that go unnoticed or avoided, as you adapt and energise your embodiment you will see the importance of peace within every experience.

The concept of a beam of light and the tree of life is a very harsh reality to swallow for those who are selective in what they see, and the jump from being locked up with your mind to a high vibrational space of alignment isn't just readily available, it always takes time. Learning and adapting as we experience the physical form. A lot of people would say if they don't see it, they can't believe it, it's an imprint of a conditioning. A mindset that relates to control, as it is easier to change rules to obtain power, as they are unable to see peace in their identity. We connect in with every awakening and spiritual moment of enlightenment, it is a constant feed of energy that gives us access to a collective network.

The vision of nature, the planet, and the universe display characteristics that our purpose is about placing your faith in your existence. A place that has gratitude and love, which accepts the moment. Once we have become in tune with a connection to a higher vibrational state we can then start participating and involving ourselves with the core principles of the universe. How we attach and harness our energy will open new doors that align with internal acceptance of evolution. We touch in with the network that gives us access to the intuitive relationship we have to our environment. A grand state of empowerment where we harness a collective stance that vibrates to the frequency of our situation. We are joined to the collective network, every time we grow a branch or a root, we are covered with blessings of the divine source that supplies us with the knowledge of our balance alignments.

When you stop and look upon your life, trying to put together the pieces of your life you will be faced with obstacles and restrictions that are deliberately placed in your way. Healing is always down to the individual and what type of life experiences they have participated in and been witness to. We can enter a stage of divine peace, an embodiment that is weightless, a moment of knowing that skeleton of energy that is connected through dimensions, through auras and across plains, that no matter what, physical manipulation is preventing people from healing. It is knowing that no matter what happens the divine light that you share represents the true meaning of peace. Sacred knowledge and wisdom are translated through an unconditional space connected to the divine languages of the collective. Gain access to the most privileged essentials for your purpose.

There are few words that describe an experience between dimensions, it is a knowing. A feeling inside of you that knows it comes from a place that's within, a divine language that is inside all of us, but we just don't know how to access it. The experience of the sacred knowledge will only ever be yours, having faith in yourself and being at peace will divinely guide you forward. Processing energies and memories are uniquely bound to your reality, and the answers you seek are already available inside of you. If you choose to acknowledge your organic energetic ability to connect in with the universe, you can move towards a place of peace and potentially when you are ready, you will open the door of higher consciousness while accessing the core principles of the universe. A door that does not have a lock, nor a handle and it is only you that can open it. This process of connecting to the divine source can take many lifetimes.

Core principles are a network that divinely connects all available energies and spaces to the divine source, knowing the workings will at some stage assist in your decision making, but for now you may have to draw your attention to the practical workings of your mind, and how you're looking back to strengthen your future.

Core Principles are the reason you can experience such a variety of valuable lessons across many different lifetimes. The network that can never be covered by books. So, when you look to understand core principles it starts with accountability, recognizing your own personal identification that is responsible for all personal growth. The belief in yourself is the only platform that gives you access as you work today in a higher place of enlightenment.

This book is about you and your health, but no matter

how much I offer guidance, your happiness is only available when you accept your true potential as you work on your mind, body, and soul. People who find themselves lost are faced with a reality that personal traits like judgement and control, remove any ability to honour themselves. The love for yourself and others is only the start as you connect in with the alignments of nature. A set of foundations that supports future generations to experience the greatest honour of their embodiment.

CHAPTER 7

INFLUENCES

Our daily routines are full of different personalities that all push their own agendas and life challenges. We are always looking to surround ourselves with like-minded people, but by failing to recognise how people are directing their use of experiences to influence each other, can easily dictate the direction of our actions. A healthy mindset knows the importance of respect, an ability that starts from the feeling of an internal understanding of the bigger picture. Through any process of identification that crosses your path you should always start by registering the feeling when you look within. Our own feelings and emotions are linked to the control of how we choose to influence ourselves and others. Past events that were avoided and/or pushed aside will accumulate or attach to an alternative source. A lack of personal identity will rely on external teachings to search for an internal understanding, but without having a basic layout of standards we will always be subject to a controlled force from others. We influence ourselves by the relationship between our actions, our thoughts, and our embodiment. The embodiment can easily be removed from the equation if either your thoughts or actions have detoured from a purpose to influence an alternative reality of disconnection.

Our personal journey towards a higher knowing of respect depends on the influential teachers within our life, people that see you and provide a space that creates the realisation of internal empowerment and peace. Knowing that it will never be about the internal struggles or conflict, but about the evolutionary understanding of how the alignment from your actions and thoughts can enlighten you. Nature provides this space of self-reflection and minimises our congestive lifestyles. Without core principles and peace, we will continue to create problems. Linking the direct actions of your internal status to the flow of transferred energy from one moment to the next, this will indicate the type of influences you are attracting. We are subjected to a huge number of controlling influences that all have their alternative motives and as we digest and reflect on the values in which people are displaying, it can either provide you with a broad understanding of the underlining conditions or can shut you down by forcing you into a closed off mindset.

The way you digest an event depends on your values. Living in a society that has distanced itself from core principles we are left with the idea that rules and regulations, while adapting to social requirements, are accepted for our best interest for our individual health. However, when moving towards the process of internal healing and understanding your identity it is hard to find a source of the values that resonate with the internal principles of respect. Leading to a confused state of disempowerment. Respect is about balance; you must be able to respect yourself to respect someone else. You may never be able to agree with their actions and thoughts, but brushing those aside, there is still a person in an embodiment that you will never be able to understand their life, so judgement is a conclusion of your own insecurities. Your understanding of respect sets the ability to evolve away from restrictions and move towards a higher understanding of their own identity.

By achieving a certain degree of respect for yourself you're able to identify and break down boundaries, the process of knowing that the respect for yourself and the problems you hold should not become part of someone else. The lack of internal control means that if I cannot understand or identify any type of influencing energies, it will circulate around your mind and body until the moment of release is available, directed towards a situation that is emotionally charged and unstable. The fixation of the controlling influence will circulate to a degree that it is constantly eating you from the inside, until a moment of outburst or expression is directed in a manner that is emotionally distressed. Even though the expression is asking for help, it's up to the individual to step forward and ask. When someone is struggling with the effects of influencing energies, it is never our place to push opinions, narrative, or form conclusions but to welcome them into a space that allows them to think freely.

Finding spiritual friends that provide a space for stages of healing is always about the unconditional space between you. Once acknowledged wisdom can be obtained when willing to listen so your voice can be heard. This is a start to any journey that recognises the importance of being free in your own mind. The comfortability of acceptance with who you are, is an attribute that supports the reality of how aligned the decisions you make, that influences the positions you hold when faced upon the difficulties of both internal and external growth. During any stage of healing, you will always be adapting and re-aligning. The pathway to unconditional and united embodiment doesn't happen overnight, lessons are learnt, ideas are processed, and events happen. The continuous repositioning of every influential event in your life with an honest and truthful review will gradually bring you onto a pathway that rings true.

The understanding of your path helps in evaluating the current influential energies you've surrounded yourself with. Dominant or important characters will have had a variety of influences during various stages of your life. As you've grown into this life, certain figures would have been accountable for the mindset that creates the way you digest your opinions. The more restrictions and controlling figures that have dominated your growth, the higher the possibility that your constructed reality is limited to other people's ideologies and intentions. Linking your status or ideologies from events or figures from the past, opens the possibility of identifying habits and routines that are not aligned on a personal account but are the creation of other origins.

Knowing where you've obtained a certain personality trait helps digest the idea of being able to understand the process it requires to heal and determines whether these influential energies are healthy for you. The personal internal review will be the first challenge to accepting past actions and choices. To break down and understand how events played out, while reviewing the teachings of others is about accountability and the way you deal with influential energies from the past, present, and future. To understand the steps you take within this moment, you first must know how you got here. Dominant figures such as parents, grandparents, friends, and teachers all have their own individual ways of influencing, all drawing from experience. The ones that have influenced you the most will have imprinted a certain type of personality trait into your ideology, a mindset that could have enlightened the path to understanding yourself or could have spread their past pain and heart ache, so it is now imprinted in the way you perceive life.

Syphoning out the energies that support your growth is all about how much you're willing to hold a space of true accountability. The past that has gone unfiltered will continue controlling the way you interact. The answers of core principles lay asleep inside waiting for a connection so it can transform to the physical form. The way you influence yourself is by a mindset that requires the transcripts from past events, displaying a set of ideologies that are vacant inside of your mind. Knowing that once a conversation starts and a certain type of topic has been triggered, your own pain could approach the forefront of your conversation and influence other people. Our default painful stance is now controlling the flow of an interaction that will soon overflow into someone else's mental display and potentially impact them with the harsh realities of your own inability to process and understand past events.

The way you enter a conversation is a test of what beliefs are resonating from within, it is also a measure of the type of situations we put ourselves in. The strength of our personal empowerment is a test of character, questioning whether we are learning or lacking our own accountability and ignoring the lessons while carrying on putting ourselves in difficult spaces. If the conversation is hard and it's stirring all types of emotionally charged feelings, the likelihood of understanding the conversation has become irrelevant and all you will end up doing is fighting against yourself, selecting what you are wanting to hear. Unhealthy influential energies are not just mentally present, but they can be triggered during multiple various stages of life, activating an internal war of pain, an unwelcome energy that controls the mind from processing simple life lessons. Having stagnant energies restricts the natural flow of learning. Without even being able to understand or recognise dominant forces from the past, our spiritual evolutionary growth is restricted or even halted due to the inability to let those energies flow freely through you.

Every choice, decision, conversation, and interaction are always open to interpretation, and depending on the personal alignment, depends on how much of the participating energies are restricted from you. Tunnel vision can cause an alternative method of how you allow yourself to receive the information. Those who have had an instrumental controlling ideology stamped on their interpretation of a certain reality will default and instantly close any ability to see beyond their own restrictions. Having tunnel vision can create a mindset that searches for power, a moment where if the energies fall within the boundaries of the limited vision, they are more likely to act and move towards those actions of control. A simple expression that avoids the reaction of accountability can push them towards the concepts of addictions. The corridor that closes the avenue to responsibility leads to the influence of believing they're in control but are only acting out someone else's reality. This sign of manipulation is common in all areas of society, especially those in younger age groups. An idea that someone who tries to teach others but is directed by fear, controls the ability of how much growth someone can gain. Repeatedly rattling the cage to restrict their ideology is a place that makes them surrender their own ability to interact with their internal expansion of being able to learn.

The influences that are outside our field of control that directly impact our daily interactions are every energy that affects you directly, but indirectly avoids their accountability of communication. We are inundated with a landslide of a passive aggressive network that is constantly attacking your state of mind. A strong mind only needs one moment of weakness to fall subject to the indirect attack that does not recognise personal boundaries. The materialistic world of technology exists on the platform that you are weak and unable to measure the value of a product that doesn't resonate with the internal alignment of your higher self. When our state of embodiment is compromised, we are typically at the will of the flow that dominates the conversation within society. Our daily interactions could soon become part of the influencing energy that has gained momentum. The concept of just accepting the narrative is one of the first signs that you have lost the power to make your own decisions, decisions that within your own reality should always be looked upon from a neutral point of view. Making calculated decisions on the energies and the information you have available, or even researching the understanding of the knowledge or motive behind this influencing energy. Our subconscious mind notices all energies that were present, and as you move towards a place of peace, you will know through your own instincts whether the energy is positive or negative.

One part of the first awakenings you may experience is the harsh understanding that the truth will set you free, but when one's reality is their truth it's then when you realise the power of offering a free space to someone. We are constantly under attack from opinions and personal motives that are emotionally charged, but the way they will try and influence you is through a lack of control. Throughout your life the way you hold yourself and interact with society is depending on the type of influential energy you offer. To be a positively influential person to close family and friends, you first must find yourself. Any problem, physical or mental, you must hold yourself accountable and stop the idea of projecting your pain out into the world. Recognising that the boundary of your empowerment supports the space you hold to influential people in a way that doesn't control their status but allows them to conclude and make their own reflection of events.

There is a tough line that is commonly mistaken, when someone is hurting and unable to contain their emotions. They may inadvertently ask for help via an expression of a negative set of comments, potentially aimed towards people that are closest to them. This is a signal that they are crying out for help as their emotions are boiling over, but within their life, their reality, they see that expression as justified, unable to recognise that it is their pain, and they are trying to ask for someone's help. If they're unknown to you, the outburst may be as simple as someone trying to find some stable ground in a search for empowerment to recognise their own self-identity. Either way these situations have an influence on you. Without being able to recognise the energies, they will go untouched, with the possibility of them soon becoming part of your own reality, until it's your turn to express how you feel to someone else.

Any energies that create a relationship that is formed on the concept they may be trusted; they match the frequency or ideology in which you want to attract. If you are lost you may find outlets to fill a space, look for happiness or an alternative view, only ending up being addicted to several types of influential energies. Once you hold onto an addictive influential energy you will never be able to see the direction in which it takes you, locked onto your reality, realising boundaries to only surrender any empowerment that is freely given to something that is attached onto a vulnerable state, a state that is now part of yourself and attached to your aura when deciding personal life choices.

No matter where you are in the world, within your direct surroundings there are influential and inspirational energies. The choice to absorb and understand the teaching on display is up to you, being in that moment, accepting the reality, is always down to your free choice. The direction in which past teachings have taken you, will have either embraced and enhanced your independence towards free choice, or would have gradually and eventually removed the collective supporting network of one's personal alignment in a stage where you are no longer in control of knowing the qualities of free choice. An energy that will always come back to the strength of how much you recognise the person you are. Avoidance will only distance yourself from the purpose of your embodiment. Our personal empowerment is influenced by the foundation that we ground and evolve as one, our lives and our journey. The world that we have created has closed off our mindset and removed basic avenues of self-healing and reflection that are linked to our own personal accountability, and the start of any process that needs the tender loving space of time knows that within that window it will come down to how much you respect the person you've become. Give an honest review whether you're in control or there is another type of power at play.

When people have the chance to let life be for a simple moment, so they can remove themselves from the picture to rebalance their aura is now a skill lost for most individuals. We are our own judge and jury when it comes to the ways you look inwards and outwards. The equation that it is simple and easy to achieve a state of divine peace is wrong, it's a complex journey and depending on how much you've ignored yourself, possibility through teachings that were out of your control such as ideologies and conditions or self-sabotaging behaviours that have been emotionally charged. It is never too late to honour yourself and look for peace, the freedom of choice is still available, even if it's only a small corner of the window that your mind is allowing you to see in this moment.

Our daily choices are the way we choose to influence ourselves. If we look to be active, eat healthily, uphold personal care for our physical and mental states and the way we interact with society. Close friends and family can open the possibility that we know that free choice is related to mental and physical conditions. Whereas if you've fallen subject to the conditioning that doesn't freely allow you space to understand that moment, you can quite easily attach your energy to a subset of underlining realities that transmute depending on their motivation of control. If your actions go unchecked you influence yourself and others, and due to the conditioned opinion of society it now believes this is the normal way to behave, you can quite easily fall subject to negative habits that disconnects reality from your ability to perform and sustain a healthy routine. Working our way through the changing conditions of society, it can be extremely difficult to distance yourself enough to create a moment of self-awareness that understands your personal boundaries. A transition that recognises the conditioning which has removed their ability to identify their own mental health status as it stays locked up in the compounds of a restricted reality.

Large parts of society are chasing an image that is false by nature and creation, an attack on your visual interpretation of how you acknowledge the world. Leaving a devastating imprint of an attitude that seeks to obtain a status of lies, it affects your relationship, your life trajectory, your mental health, and your innate ability to be at peace. The image of perfection covers a false narrative that encourages you to give up your happiness in a goal that only serves the materialistic market. A single word, perfect, is like searching for an equal, it doesn't exist. The quality and unique vibrational realities of balancing the world is on the principle that each separate frequency adds to the collective of a divine life. You attach energies and align sources that match, but not equal, the frequencies that harmonise with every energy has its own individual imprint.

If your fairy tale is on the grounds that you are only wanting an image that is sold by movies, or advertising or even projected ideologies, you are step away from looking from within that allows you to search for a connection that completes you. Every decision or conflict that requires attention, is never about looking for the answers that people expect of you, but about knowing that your happiness is directly connected to your health and wellbeing as you move towards an environment where people respect the values as you turn your attention to working on your mind, body and soul.

People who seek to gain control of others are doing so not because they can't release control, but because they've lost the freedom of their control. At some stage of their life their powers of freewill have been removed and taken away from their embodiment.

The world of influences are direct targets to predetermine your past, present and future. Your world of freedom will never exist if you can't recognise the power of your own mind. A lost soul that is searching to find its way through challenging times, will start the process of healing if you recognise the repeating pattern to self-sabotage your own happiness. A behavioural pattern that will always be at the expense of your physical and mental health.

CHAPTER 8

MEDITATION

No matter what stage of your personal spiritual journey you are currently processing, the bond and connection from your actions, choices and decisions play a critical part in how much you are embracing your purpose for this lifetime. Processing in the moment events can become tedious and hard for a logical brain. The logical part of our teaching can function as a highly restrictive consequence for rejecting basic intuition and natural instincts. Given that the current structure requires certain conditions on how you're meant to behave and interact with other people, predetermining a repetitive reaction of coming to conclusion an event prior to even evaluating the circumstances.

To compress the growth that is part of you and to remove the honour of being enlightened a logical mind sets and creates conditionings on how you process any decision-making moments, while calculating a risks and rewards formula to receive the greatest materialistic outcome. Overall logic hinders and restricts the full evaluation of any event. It doesn't allow for the structure of your internal and external gifts. It sets boundaries and draws conclusions based on past traumas, which categories areas that simplify decisions. Removing all areas that require feelings and emotions while influencing in the way we participate to avoid. The expansion of greed and wealth formed a limited zone that only allows certain types of opinions and narratives to be present. Narratives that have removed the functionality and basic life essentials of making caring and loving decisions only to know that your success or failure is on the back of someone else's pain. Lessons and beliefs that are built into our life from the moment we are created, as the manipulation of the logical brain removes the existence of the unseen and unknown due to the fear and lack of control in a system that requires both conditions to operate.

The transfer of the logical brain to a meditational state is one of the principal areas of restrictions that you will experience when trying to connect to a deeper part of your soul. The chances are that you've sacrificed yourself and your personal journey to be accepted in society. Even at an early age, your parents would be making sacrifices to a cause they don't really understand. Unable to teach you anything about yourself, but only the lessons that were taught to them, a chain that locks the shackles around your purpose.

As the logical brain has evolved, it now needs a constant injection of information to sustain the production of an addictive state, and as it is unable to process or interpret anything outside its own set of parameters, an alternative reality that removes the basic life essentials of downtime or personal freedoms. It cannot operate through the connective network of the universe, a knowing that feelings or emotions are identifying the areas beyond the unknown, to only calculate and disregard the conclusion of your purpose.

There is no denying that logic is an essential part of our brain. It has provided us with the ability to be innovative which has helped design and construct all parts of modern-day society, but as our journey of completion requires involving our whole strength of the embodiment, the logical brain only fulfils a small percentage of who we are. The idea that our current existence is operating entirely on a formatted logical conclusion supports the reality that we are failing to identify key and essential qualities of being part of this life.

There is a degree of heightened efficiency where a logical format in an evolutionary period is necessary but everything after that has an ability to cause a negative reaction. A chain of events that is likely to spiral as it is unable to stabilise into a reliable source.

Dedicating all your energy to a logical mindset creates a tunnel vision and with that tunnel vision it encourages the deceit of a lost mind to believe it is optimising the productivity of its own efficiency, just like a conveyor belt in a factor. When you've been in this zone and maintain a constant flow of life by participating in this logical formula, it soon becomes hard to think outside of that reality, as you believe this is the normal. There is a huge amount of resistance that will prevent even the smallest of changes, and you will go to great lengths to convince yourself that you're happy, stable and that you must work hard to move forward in life. Reiterating to yourself that it's all about how productive your day is, as you measure the materialistic wealth on how successful your life has become.

As you move towards a place of self-care and internal happiness you will be faced with the default stance of your conditioning, that restricts your advancements of being able to hold a space. We have designed a logical system that is now doing more harm than good. Within your limited window the aspect of evolving must be logical, this condition does not allow you to identity the soul to its embodiment, as your worth is the value of what you add economically to the system. At the start of digesting life outside of religious beliefs we created a formula that took its information scientifically or mathematically in an idea to understand the overall purpose of the scientific and economic communities. The evolution of the logical mind, but because of the efficiency in which it requires for a logical platform, the performance must be under certain set of conditions. It has taken away our own ability to identify, we rely so much on this structure that it erases every possibility that is blessed beyond those limitations. Economically for individuals to have emotions and feelings, while fulfilling a peaceful and happy life is not practical, it applies the opposite effect of what must be achieved when reviewing a materialistic market.

As we process looking at a healthy meditational period of self-care, we must be able to identify the energies that control our actions. The notion that you can sit down and instantaneously attract the space of a higher consciousness with a limited understanding of your own journey, is extremely rare. Part of the meditational state is not just the time that you've dedicated to different qualities and aspects of your life, but it's everything before that. You must nurture the relationship of your logical brain and the rest of your embodiment. It's not as easy or as simple as flicking a switch and success is achieved.

During our day we are repositioning and relocating our stance as we are constantly transferring the interchangeable energies. This transfer on a logical controlled personality will only be open to recognising a certain type of energy with which it is familiar. To introduce another energy means the constructive design must operate outside the programming, a reality that will come with highly resistive barriers.

The process of self-healing means you're moving towards a place of oneness, which recognises your presence within the moment. Start off by self-identifying in the moment, means you can form a communication link towards an open mind, this can be achieved by combining both aspects of your brain in one bubble. Merging two different realities into one, nurturing your logical routine and inspiring the structure to evolve by introducing feelings and emotions. When we look at the two different qualities that are naturally built inside your embodiment, the second part of the bubble is an area that the logical mind cannot explain. Remembering the answer to your wholeness and inner peace is never to fight but to embrace your existence.

To think outside of logic, you must start acknowledging personal abilities and gifts that have always been present. You must start small and build a solid foundation. The balance of your embodiment recognises that you have both feminine and masculine traits built by design. When digesting and reflecting on your feelings and emotions, the awareness that at various times you will be required to process the event via different constructs and quality of alternative energies. Meaning that adapting to the balancing requirements need to be able to process both masculine and feminine energies. Understanding your alignment with the balancing principles of the universe.

The pre-meditation state allows you to set the platform in which you recognize and set boundaries for how your logical mind operates. A deeper consciousness of respect for your embodiment. If you don't open a space and you let fear, anxiety, stress, and other logical traits left unchallenged and unrecognised it will cross over and confuse other essential parts of your presence.

The most important part of meditation is the relationship within your mind that goes into a relaxed state. An ideology that ignores their daily routine is a restrictive mindset that expects a carefree and lazy attitude when focusing on their mental health. Being aware of your daily interactions and experiences means you can recognise welcoming and supporting energies that will accompany you during states of higher vibrations.

When you're preparing yourself prior to dedicating a space for a place of honour, it is the preparation that sets the tone to how much respect you have for yourself before acknowledging and opening essential health and wellbeing spaces. This process can be achieved at any time leading up to a controlled state of meditation, a period of self-love where you can review the experiences that have led to teachings across all interchangeable transfers of energy. This period of reflection could be walking the dog, on the bus home or even eating a snack. If you can enter a state of reflection without external influences compromising the realigning of the values within the lessons.

Review your day, break down moments by walking yourself through all integrated and individualised steps, and as it plays out identify the spaces, recognise the moment when one space closes and another one opens. Within each space across all events evaluate your actions and how you responded. Once this is achieved you can then move forward and digest all other energies that were present. Daily interactions can hold a lot of power over you, even if it's something as basic as a passing comment. To introduce a short cut picture to how your day played out helps to remove the direct influencing energies in an external overview of all the logical and social interactions in which you have participated. Once you have remembered the order and event in which they played out, now attach your feelings and emotions to the moments where a change in energy stands out.

Recognising that experiencing feelings and emotions is normal but being able to link those reactions to certain energies or personalities allows you to think outside of logical reasoning.

During initial stages of healing, you just want to start off by linking daily habits and routines together, breaking down your personality, opinions, reactions and if or how your terminology changes depending on if the environment is friendly or is subject to conflict.

As you've made your way through the layout in which you remember the interchangeable transactions of events, you can now start moving towards a period that crosses over from one internal ability to the next. By registering your feelings and emotions, you can highlight and detail certain times where triggers or the influential energies have shaped your personality into an alternative state. You can then highlight areas of empowerment, but if you detect a shift in your personality that moves away from core principles it can indicate that you've been subjected to a change in direction that pushes you away from being able to identify yourself within the moment. As you grow within your embodiment the ability to instantaneously reflect on events is understood within the moment, knowing that your values resonate with the action and core principles that are reflected in your personality.

Entering the state of reviewing your daily exchanges of transferable energy is communicating across both your conscious and subconscious minds. The logical format typically ignores the subconscious, as this area of the brain recognises and understands all energies that are vibrating across your aura. Our empowerment and self-identity requires us to nurture a positive attitude when merging two parts of our embodiment with one bubble, a space that holds an internal place of self-awareness. A trail of your thoughts that do not come from the conscious mind, it is a place of a feeling that cannot be explained or digested by logic. It is also your anchor, a point of reference when you activate self-acknowledgment, as it will hold a barrier of self-love that will remember to enlighten you from any resistance of the logical mind, a pattern where it will try and fight back against the period of self-care in a meditational state.

The areas of our life that are linked to the subconscious vibrational alignments are when events happen, and it resonates throughout your core. Experiences of love, happiness, freedom, and peace can all activate and enlighten our embodiment, a memory that is built into your experiences. Memories of the purest alignments are ones that logic tries to ignore, so when you're searching for memories that come from a space of love, it can act as your reference to know that there's more to this world by honouring this space of self-love that resonates from an internal part of you. When your love is attached to another energy, person, place, nature, or animal this is also another source of energy that unlocks your vision as you look towards a place of happiness. It is not one that looks to control you but a space of unconditional alignment. An energy that will ground you, as you honour yourself.

At the beginning you may find it difficult to look beyond what you've been taught, but to start with the understanding that there's a place of peace if you're willing to look outside the designed restrictions. To be able to close logic and open a window of self-care you must state your empowerment, and finish on a personal identity that you recognise as a strength. This statement is memory, or a feeling, which is linked to your emotions. A part of you that holds a certain experience close to your heart. A love or memory so strong that can support the second part of the bubble that overpowers and removes any logical control. Using this to ground you, support you and a place of reference as you look towards a sacred place within your mind.

Once this direction and empowerment has been stamped, a simple phrase, action, thought or an internal acknowledgement of a feeling that can be called upon in honour of self-care and wellness to activate the energies of being able to hold an internal space. An innate ability to clear the mind will ground the foundations for your physical body, allowing your consciousness to be free to work outside the limitations of our logical mind. As you acknowledge this space it recognises the empowerment of your anchor, and it knows when you enter this space it registers and honours a sacred moment of respect.

A meditational state is an acknowledgement of your gifts. The most well-known state of meditation is the platform of yoga, a mind and body experience where if you're looking to filter and realign to a higher place of consciousness, while supporting your body and allowing you to release blockages, it encourages your mind to work freely outside your physical experience. It has many different healing properties that are essential to everyday alignment of a higher purpose.

The concept that to enter a meditational state you must be able to work in a particular type of space and energy is very mistaken. Meditation is accessed throughout any of our abilities, a connection that links to the expansive supporting collective of the energetic network. You can move into a meditative state at any stage of the day, just by accessing your gifts and can create a link to the collective network.

With the natural flow of energy being removed we hold onto traumatic events of the past, this stumps our direct ability to heal when faced with future problems. We buckle up trying to bury those painful moments deep inside so we can avoid their existence.

Meditation is just one form that assists in being able to heal on the deepest level. Every past painful memory left untouched can control our actions in future endeavours. The expansion of your mind starts off with being open to healing. Once a healing process has been undertaken you can then move forward to aligning yourself with a set of core principles that resonate with your mind, body, and soul. Looking at the state of meditation under a particular image that it carries a place of avoidance or to follow an image that is trending, means you're not doing it for yourself to be able to heal, but under the illusion that you're trying to trick yourself and others. The relationship between your thoughts and actions is always a point of reference of how much you are honouring your health and wellbeing.

Opening your world to a life beyond the ideologies that you have been taught means that at any stage of healing it'll require you to take a step back to be able to step forward. From the first breakdown of detailing your day to the time you commit to a state of meditation, you can link the energy of freedom beyond your logical control. Once you've attached the statement that holds the caring, loving principles of your life this will anchor as your grounding point of gratitude to allow a deeper part of yourself to be free. The temptation and resistance to drift will be strong and will look to cloud your mind with excuses to avoid participation, as there is no logical benefit to it. The statement that was close to your heart will allow a window and purpose to look beyond that avoidance, open your mind to receiving and knowing that whatever message is presented, that there is wisdom attached to it. Mediation is not a place of avoidance; you don't need to enter a state if you're already choosing to escape from life.

CHAPTER 9

LEADERSHIP AND ECONOMY

A critical part of our journey and across all lifetimes is about surrounding ourselves with a community that holds and respects the collective beliefs of the universe, as it resonates to our internal values of enlightenment. One of the hardest parts of the initial stages of awakenings is that it can trigger the realisation of the truth, and a place of freedom where we can question simple concepts of how we got to this stage in humanity. Knowing that the truth isn't about blame but about understanding how and where things went wrong, so future generations can learn from our mistakes.

The trajectory in which materialistic countries must maintain a certain level of constant growth in the economy has now reached a stage that has become uncontrollable. There is no way for the platform to change its stance as the moment it fails to obtain these sets of standards, the entire system will collapse. This is an addictive state of greed and control.

The operation for the system to stabilise requires a few conditions that cannot alter away from the path it has chosen. The economic market stabilises on the constant growth of the population. It needs a small percentage of people to provide the innovative grounds for inventions for the new materialistic growth within the market. To achieve the rapid transformation of the idea where from the moment it is designed and the period that it's made available for the market, it needs a workforce that completes a certain number of hours to produce the products, in accordance with the companies that influence the design and direction of the economy.

The design of the political structure will then fall in line with the direction the market has chosen to undertake, allocating stocks, rules, and regulation in support of the financial growth of a country.

When one party is changed in the political stance of the house, they will adapt their ideology in which way the money flows. Without backing or investment they are unable to implement proposed suggestions to the public. The supporting influence of the financial market can narrate what is displayed or even hidden to the public. For the entire system to work it must supply a minimum turnover that allocates the number of jobs, new builds and structures that are being built and supplying services to all essential areas of the country. The area that has the biggest influence on where the market is performing, is the idea that they are provided with modern day luxury and essential accessories, only to have an alternative motive on their agenda.

Without that market the big company will fail to exist. They rely on most of the population to be dependent on housing, services and adding financial backing for the government, to invest back into the financial sector that they require to stay in power. It is essential for the economy that most people stay poor or within a certain limitation. They provide all the hours for production while almost all their earnings from their wages are indirectly put back into the system for external markets. A mortgage in which someone takes out will be paid over a period that could be anything up to thirty years. This locks down most people to be financially bound within their movement and powerless for their voice to be heard.

If the general population weren't kept in that financially vulnerable position, they would gradually move away from long hours and concentrate on areas of their life where they could move towards an enjoyable lifestyle. With the decrease in hours, the whole of the country would fail to function. A wealthy population is bad for the economy, as they need to be able to maintain a highly populated community for constant growth. Most of the people must stay within the limits of what they are allowed to achieve within this life. People on average will pay their mortgage back several times before they're freed from their contract, keeping their restrictions at the mercy that they've invested everything they have in this house, which the system knows is their vulnerability.

A house is much more than a thirty-year debt, it's a home. It's where the joy of experiencing life, birthing families, celebrations, freedoms, peace, and a place to escape the troubled structure of a society. The memories of a life are built within people's homes, with love and harmony setting the foundations of being able to feel free and knowing that there's more to life than work. The happiness that is available by creating a home is always a goal for most people who want to share their life experiences with others. If a large section of the community would pay mortgages back over a shorter period, it doesn't synchronise to the drums of the economy. Anyone who knows the true value of a home, will choose to spend more time with their loved ones than being made to work in support of a false reality. Minimising their hours, or changing careers early, or following a path that rings true to their heart would mean that the market doesn't have the next generation of people available to take over.

The economy survives on the basis that you're not in touch with your feelings. A person who can identify the true meaning of life is hard to control. They hold core principles and values that are not welcome in the current structure of the economy, as the economy demands that you are entirely dependent on it. A disconnected soul is a chance to profiteer, and large parts of the economy rely on you to be vulnerable in areas of your mental and physical health.

When you're emotionally charged you act irrationally in your decision making, trying to control your actions but end up being vulnerable as it reflects in your mental state. The economy makes it so that cheap food is readily available but it's unhealthy, pushing your ability to ignore the signs of addictions that causes both your physical and mental health to be compromised, and destabilising your

decision-making process. Making the way to be reliant on drugs and other areas of consumption that are just another alternative source of addiction. Large parts of the economy profiteer on your state of being disconnected from your embodiment. Pushed to the limit by your financial strain, maxed out on paying a long-term commitment, you then are typically left with no other choice but to purchase the cheaper range of items.

As the economy changes depending on the narrative and which market is set to make the most financially stable investment, your understanding of principles and beliefs will never be able to be maintained if you follow the direction in which political and financial objectives are decided. You are free if you don't ask questions outside of what they believe. Financial motives insist that the truth is too hard to handle, because spiritually, the truth will set you free.

The structure of the economic system is approaching a point in which it is about to collapse. You only have to look at the debt countries have accumulated trying to maintain this abusive mental reality. Only to end up struggling in the payments of the interest, never mind being able to pay off the full amount of debt. They have taken advantage of every soul within their reach to only let the end product collapse in front of your eyes, leading the way for only the rich to survive until next time. If the collapse in the economic market doesn't benefit the agenda that people own homes, you will not be allowed to purchase one. A type of control that has served its purpose.

Energetically how this sits within the world we must look back at the origins in which democracy was born. Democracy means the voice of the people, a mistake before it even took off. Humans for all their positive traits, left to their own devices with no understanding of core principles become selfish, irrational, angry, aggressive and many other controlling attributes. The life within this planet has never been about humanity. Left unaccountable we will slowly destroy what is not ours in a position that lacks internal peace to gain control of others. In Greece pre-democracy, there were a select number of lords that owned most of the land. Within those powers they were self-elected to control the rest of the nearby society. The powers of one life were in the hands of a group of people that controlled everything as far as the eyes can see. Questioning how a select few individuals gained or inherited power over everyone is not the direct question, but the strength of their mind with what kind of influencing control they wanted was more relative. The characters of the people in control.

Every person within the community was dictated to. They owned nothing and they had to farm the land, only to pay their profit back in taxes to the rich. The chamber of self-elected lords was not interested in understanding the reality of the people but were only interested in the control of which the power gave them. A cycle in which the rich profiteer on the labour of the poor.

Once the people stood up and questioned the abusive nature in which they were conditioned to experience, it was bloody, brutal and went on for a while. The idea that a select few people would give up control to release it back to the people was never going to happen. To allow an individual to become educated was a danger to the controlling principle in which they operated.

All trades, taxes, and cycles in which the structure was designed required people to be weak and hold no power. After a while they decided to grant the people a voice in a narrative that gave them false intentions, a trap where they believed their voice could be heard, a changing point that only altered the direction in which they gained control was now in motion. Our life is not about conflicts, it's about being at peace with the balancing qualities of the planet. You can see first-hand in modern day society when politicians are debating, their goal isn't about peace, or bringing a mutual respect for life to the chamber. It is about dressing down the opposition, making them feel small so others can gain power. A passive aggressive attitude that does not know the true value of life.

Peace will never be available if you allow humans rules and regulations to be the judge, jury, and executioner. We will never be able to recognise the truth, never mind understand it. Values and core principles must be aligned to the understanding of the planet and the universe. Energetically we are approaching a time in life that democracy will no longer be available. The universal cycle of energy is now approaching its realignment of karmic balancing, the true intentions of which the deception was created under is now about to reveal itself. The democracy umbrella was never truly available under the image we believed it existed, only by those deceitful few to gain and seek control, an attitude that was driven by greed and had no intention to be at peace with the planet. Their real motives have always been about power, greed, and control.

We are approaching an era where communication and technology will be a topic that influences people in a variety of diverse ways. Those who look to gain control over people will use technology in a way that is formulated by a controlled digital stamp. Pushing the boundaries of your ability to self-identity in a picture that does not allow you to make personal choices. No matter what is developed, the underlining message of respect is that it should never be used to control you, but only there to support you. Those who are willing to look outside their logical reasoning and move towards a peaceful life will try to implement technology, so it supports the environment and matches the balancing frequencies of the planet. To look after the planet, we must recognise people's mental health, a direction that involves releasing all control and manipulation so we can set the foundation for an advanced society that does not seek to control.

Identifying the good in an era that grows on pain can open new doors, to a long-term success where we are able to live peacefully within your sacred places. Lessons can be learnt, and teachings should be taught, books should be written, all supporting a higher purpose so that we don't continue repeating the same mistakes over and over again.

The economy relies on international trade, and the biggest creators of pollution are wars, ships, and planes. All these are essential to the way the economy grows, it relies upon the way you can remove the ability for a country to become independent. When countries realise all values of their independence for a materialistic political stunt, they are releasing their freedom and the citizens identity, while ignoring science and the true purpose of the land they reside in.

For science to evolve into its purest form, it is within the same breath that we need to heal, this is a joint venture connecting with the expansive network of the universe. A journey that will not happen overnight, it will take years for humans to heal or even understand the pain they brought on themselves. What individualised work the countries do now will help rebuild their energetic connection to the grounds they call home. It will then start a process of achieving their own independent identity that is united across all spaces, as it moves forward it will strengthen the people and help future generations.

A world where the economy is one of a few driving forces that does not allow the people to fulfil their own purpose within this life, our restrictions have now controlled the calling where the logical brain cannot evolve as one with the rest of the mind, body, and soul. It fails with the basic principles of self-care and the deepest form of healing. We must start allowing ourselves to heal and open our minds as we expand our potential and embrace the purest form of our existence. If this is not recognised, the logical mind will seek by design to destroy. You will only ever be known as a number as the value of your mental and physical health will only ever be placed within the picture frame.

When we look at the design of the system, of how it got to this position it's clear it's no one's fault. People have adapted to survive in an environment that does not hold values. The formula that moulded the economic evolution believes that there is no other way of achieving the levels of this current stage that humans have accomplished, without pain or people suffering, it's all part of the system. It is the only system they know; they are designed by default to not think outside of the parameters of the logical economic environment.

When you look within, you cannot hide away from personal past experiences, and you hold yourself accountable as you process areas of your life that have been heavily subjected to conditioning. An attitude of being lazy or carefree is no longer an option because you have a purpose. The past is your judge if you choose to avoid it. The idea of healing will stop due to the fear of avoidance and your inability to self-identity and recognise the blessings that have been hidden from you.

The framework in which the political system is always changing, highlights areas of confusion not evolution. When you have a group of officials that change their values depending on the economy, they lack the idea of principles. A reality which indicates a controlled mindset that is built on the premises we can only operate on the short term. Knowing that it has never been about upholding rules that are based on the longevity of the people's health but implementing a false concept that your voice counts. The respect for your mental state is irrelevant because it doesn't give them power. They require votes, and their victory is based on the likelihood that just as many people do not support them, as those that voted for them.

A person lost, holds their value in the amount of money they earn or in the materialistic items that they have purchased. When looking for guidance they search for those they believe are the best influence for their lives, but a government only looks short term due to the framework of the economy. A designed reality that the people within the community only value the short-term ideology. A narrative that reflects across all aspects of their life, they don't understand the meaning of long-term abundance, so when faced upon relationship or personal problems, it is easier to start again, purchase new, and avoid their feelings. The message from any political establishment must always represent the health and the land of the people before any economy that influences us domestically or overseas. The value of money should be never greater than the physical and mental health of the citizens, we currently have those principles the wrong way around. Branches of deceit that continue pushing narratives while supporting the picture that gives them the most power.

There are many clever and intelligent people who work hard through training and have reached a certain level of a specialised skill. A lot of professionals work their whole career chasing personal recognition. Stemming from a local to a global level, it is all individualised to their personal life journeys. The development of science is highly abused for personal gain, pushing the boundaries across foundational principles that are unnatural and do not align to the divine balancing of the planet. Offering a space to a skilled individual and allow them the chance to create or invent something that synchronises to those principles, will only ever support future generations and the planet.

Science and its true evolutionary path are halted by egos that beat to the drums of the economy, a mindset that cannot see the light, or even recognise the value of life. We are moving towards a time where our principles and designs must align with the healing of the planet. A state of respect, a platform to evolve with peace in our hearts. When we look at mental health and connect it with nature, we can move towards the expansive consciousness that is linked to the mind. There are only rules and regulations in which professionals research and develop their ideas, a reality that does not know the value of the divine core principles of the universe. Wisdom that can only be obtained when you set simple boundaries of accountability and responsibility for one's life.

For science to feel goes against everything that is developed in the economy. Our embodiment and recognition of the soul isn't about books nor papers, but it's a feeling that comes from within, a sacred space that opens new avenues to welcome in various sources of collective energies, a reality which the logical mind cannot operate under. Lessons and teachings that cannot be fully understood from reading a book, nor telling people how to act. We have a natural language that gives up access to the collective vision of the planet. We have libraries that support the growth of logic consumption but now it is time to know our journey starts with accessing and accepting life beyond restrictions, a reality that uses logic in support of freedom. A statement that sees mental health and knows the core principles of life.

Our values and principles are directly linked to how someone offers a space and allows them to align their vibrational wholeness. Imagine an advanced species that understood the lessons of freedom as they worked to protect and support the aligning energies of nature. Logic left unchecked should never be used and developed without principles, a history of individual minds that left alone have already recorded a lot of wisdom that have been discovered. Our journey should not use individual inventions or the discoveries for greed so others can use it for control. Our methods need a point of reference, a collective alignment where its developed and supported in the right environment, one that acknowledges the abilities of the collective mind that grows into their embodiment, and then science and technology would take a clean and pure path once it supports the balancing energies of the universe.

Rules and regulations left unchecked create more red tape, a design feature to avoid accountability, so no one can understand the truth. A system that leaves egos to push boundaries and expand the deceit of how knowledge is communicated throughout the community. We then are digesting a consumption of lies with a small part of the aligning truth, as they form their narrative to move agendas from point to point. We don't hold beliefs, nor do we represent loyalty or trust, a system that cannot operate with those principles as our economy needs the majority of people to be weak and vulnerable when open to suggestive ideas. A method that uses a drip system to allocate a select message to the public, hiding the motive behind the deceit. People are paid to lie, argue, avoid accountability, and push narratives, it is the foundation of the economic structure.

When we look at our own state of mental and physical health it's about honour, an appreciation for life and others. Through any stage of enlightenment, we look to surround ourselves with welcome and positive energies. You can find these qualities in people if you look at the world through your eyes and honour yourself while speaking the truth about how leaders and the economy works. A place of harmony that understands an honest state of reflection. Being honest and accountable starts when you look at how you operate within the parameters of your own world. Until you know the type of energy you want to attract, you'll always be subject to lies and manipulation from all areas of the community.

CHAPTER 10

EGOS AND TRIGGERS

As we move through life, we may find ourselves in many difficult and uncomfortable positions. No matter how big or small these may seem, a deeper knowledge on how you cope with processing key moments will carve your own personality, an image displaying a characteristic in how you want the world to see you. Everyone has an ego, it is a mind's understanding of how we have dealt with our own life's experiences that is reflected in our own personality, an internal space that's projected as an image of what we want people to see. Egos are normally spoken about in a context that is typically described as a negative form. Of your own actions in difficult situations, actions that are formed by experience and have shaped the path of your own personal trajectory in this world.

A lot of people will experience moments when our ego is bruised or hurt, this doesn't necessarily mean you have done something wrong, it's just a change of situation that you will have had to adapt to. For example, if you're bubbly and friendly and always like to see the positive in something, at some stage you may potentially meet someone with a negative mindset who will show signs of a sharp tongue, with the ideology that projects and aimed at targets to inflict some type of painful expression resulting in your ego being hurt and bruised. A situation that no one should be subjected to. Emotionally charged and angry people rely on others to carry their pain. However, with your journey it's how you move on that really highlights your true character. Every moment contains a secret message that is there to help you, you've just got to find it and understand it. A positive and upbeat attitude that is open to true self-reflection can eventually lead to a spiritual ego and higher form of connection. We do not actively seek bad situations to work out the good, otherwise you're driven by the reality of looking for painful events.

Throughout your life, your ego has been built up over all your past experiences. It can stem from a wide range of distinct types of influencing energies like beliefs, relationships, pain, and anger. The lack of teachings to understand painful events can create loops where you keep repeating the same habits and routines. Due to ideologies, beliefs and conditioning, these traits sadly affect large numbers of the population. Not knowing their own character abilities, personality, skills, and empowerment, they find themselves being driven by an ego that has adapted to suit society. Relationships are a classic example of continuing to commit to a certain type of person that doesn't resonate with your soul. People will display a beacon that matches the aura that you want to attract, and you mimic the displayed characteristics as part of your personality. A relationship that is built on false intentions as they search to find themselves. Neither of these people are to blame, they have their own history and story to tell, but they have reached a point that they are purely committing and aligned to a false reality of each other.

The same concept is applied to friendship groups and social circles. Depending on your own history you will either attract a certain quality in a friend or disconnect from making friendships in general. As social trends evolve you may find social groups and friends that are continuing to change their personality ego to adapt with the needs of society. These transactions can be difficult and painful to watch, and we are never really taught how to understand energies of how we are influenced into living on autopilot and disconnecting from our souls. Personality egos that struggle with the grey area of self-identity can form and design certain characteristics in personalities that are subjected to the society's conditioning. Personality traits like depression, anxiety, disconnect, laziness and lack of motivation, all adapt to a way that exists on a change of ego in a moment. Never truly understanding the innate abilities of their own empowerment.

Even though there are many types of conditionings that are displayed in your ego, there is one expression of ego that it is created through design. The world survives on ambitious, motivated, and intelligent young promising individuals that have a point to prove, an image of materialistic wealth that is imprinted in a reality that pushes a certain concept in how someone should seek to gain wealth and fortune. Smartly dressed, presentable, holds an image of success in their materialistic items. Nice cars, watches, suits, and handbags are all items that are pushed by advertising to target a select few individuals for all of society to witness. The targeted individuals have chosen a career in the corporate market, an ambition that is either through personal success in education or via motivation from their family. A creation of the ego that helps avoid accountability for those who earn profits, but the nature in which the ego is conditioned exists on the rules that it's a dangerous world and only the fittest survive.

A world where feelings and emotions don't exist. The amount of people who push for promotions and success are itching to move up the ladder and will prove themselves at any level. The middle managers are a blame game, and they are introduced by design so those who make the money are not faced with the accountable acts and place themselves in a position of avoidance towards any questionable consequences that affect employees. During stages of restructuring, they are the first to be removed and replaced with a different title.

A designed ego that just does not stop within the workplace, but it spreads and evolves around society, for young and old that is subject to a harsh hitting reality of an ego to avoid accountability. For those young ambitious people who do not have a family or moved away from family for their job, they get entangled in the lines between a forced ego that requires them to treat the world as replaceable and irrelevant, and the idea that having feelings and emotions is a conflicting part of their existence.

Humans design and construct all types of egos. Our economy designs diverse types of negative influential egos to profiteer on their disconnected reality, as their agenda uses lost souls while concluding their purpose as replaceable. Those who are subjected to these conditions soon see the world through the eyes of their employer. People and friends become replaceable with no value; they treat life as a hierarchy, placing themselves at the top to gain the most control over any situation. If they have been introduced to this world before they have started having a family, there will be stages of a triggered ego. The way they address public and close friends in close contact moments of transferable energy where communication is teaching a projected ideology that affects all areas of the society. With children, schools, sporting events, confrontational debates all directed towards vulnerable targets as their reality creates self-inflicted moments of passive aggressive projections that dominate the atmosphere of other people's minds. Taking advantage of people that are still trying to find their way within the world.

With the constraints of their position, they are required to change characteristics of their designed personality in which they target and portray a unique style of influencing ego to achieve success. They are charming, very persuasive, but very untrustworthy and will say what they need to, to get forward. They become incredibly attractive when they want to stamp their signature of power, a philosophy that is carved into their reality by the routine tasks they are required to undertake. They beat the drums of wars as they have failed to hold values or principles in how you should treat other people with underlining respect and appreciation.

It is the overflow in which this carved ego has taken form in targeting people when they are in a vulnerable state. A person who is subjected to a controlling energy naturally builds a defensive stance of self-protection. However, if you dedicate a large amount of time and energy defending yourself, you can soon easily become what you avoid or despise, stamping an image of how to gain power over attacking someone. The state in which your vulnerability defends from aggressive egos, can within a moment of weakness become part of our own personality in a direction that has lost touch with their relationship of their own empowerment as they seek and gain power from others.

A person struggling to self-identify their purpose that lacks self-control will use methods they have visually witnessed or been subjected to where a character displays an overreach towards someone else's personal boundaries. A lost soul struggling to understand themselves can soon confuse their existing ideology to participate in their own overreach of power, aimed at attacking in a confused search of trying to understand their feelings as they lack control and identity. This transfer of energy starts with greed and spreads throughout all the communities that have had an influential motive in a materialistic platform, as it only understands one language, and it achieves wealth with no boundaries.

The only way a design ego can attack people's freedoms is by targeting a place of disconnection that infiltrates their personal physical and mental state. A planned event in which the planet now encourages personality traits and behaviours on how communities should interact with each other. The end goal is always to increase profit margins, but as they target sectors, they accelerate the contamination process of people's ideology that ends up reflecting and exposing all communities.

The design ego is destructive by nature, but no matter how much you have been influenced by the controlling energy, there is always a window of self-reflection, a single message that you receive from your consciousness about your past actions. Ignored, they will carry on as previously, but when you can sense the outcome, it can start creating internal struggles. There's an internal battle that happens when you are not taught how to process events within the moment, a fight between yourself and a reality that is becoming part of yourself. The idea that the strong survive, meaning you should fight the internal conflict, is a conclusion that has never been able to register the caring and loving effects of finding inner peace. You can never fight yourself, only understand the energies and allow the purest form of internal peace that aligns with the planet and the core principles of the universe.

An ego is an internal reflection of the type of powers that either control you or set you free, a logic conclusion never allows you the freedom to work outside the restriction parameter of the materialistic wealth, but to be able to move forward towards finding peace. An ego that completes an embodiment knows that whatever test of character there's a divine link to an unconditional source that protects our existence beyond this dimension. The moment of knowing that our egos represent the higher knowledge of peace, harmony and love that are connecting across all energies within the universe.

Everybody has moments where certain energies, personalities, events, or situations have caused so much emotional pain that the default training stance from your logical reaction is to ignore, or if advised to forget about it. An answer that is repeated time and time again, across all walks of society, as people struggle to cope with their own problems. They are at a loss when offering advice to someone else who is in an emotionally controlled state. The repetitive categorisations of avoidance and trying to forget will soon start to eat you from the inside. Holding copious amounts of unprocessed emotional experiences inside your body, blocking organic and positive energy from trying to flow through you. The system sets you up to fail, leaving people in such a vulnerable state that they will soon search out avenues that can release the pain and burdens trapped inside of them. These avenues are typically a physical form of reaction, trying to escape the reality that is present inside their mind and body causing a negative physical and/or verbal state of pain, consequently leading to states of addiction.

The lines in which certain negative and uncontrollable egos have effect over you, will depend on whether you have been bullied or are the bully. Either form of encounters create indirect triggers that can be imprinted on your aura from as little as a couple of days old. The energy of your past trauma that controls your actions, opinions and life theories are displayed within your beliefs. As simple as talking to someone can highlight your fears and indicate what is currently in control of the mindset that dominates your present trail of thoughts.

Beliefs that are manipulated from fear are methods in which people can control you. A simple trigger can redirect your trail of consciousness to a place that motivates you to seek alternative methods to avoid places of unprocessed energetic realities. The unprocessed experiences can and will lead to addiction if unable to understand the source of the energy that you are trying to avoid. Triggers themselves, moves your mind and body away from self-identity in a place of disconnection that pushes the lack of empowerment towards an expression that is consumed on substantial amounts of unprocessed and unrecognised energies.

Triggers are unprocessed stagnant energetic experiences that can control you daily and change your reality in moments where we are unable to understand the internal struggles of our external reactions. Every part of our active lives can be compromised by the event of triggering a chain reaction of a combination of past experiences. The past is a place that needs revisiting to be able to walk forward. Forms of the deepest type of healing require understanding sources where triggers were attached and have influenced your foresight and the ability to make daily choices that align to the highest form of consciousness. If you allow triggers to go unnoticed, they will continue attaching to the chain of reactions, making your life complicated. A variety of different sources can trigger a variety of different outcomes, leaving your state in a complete dismantling of any available space to be in the moment.

Physiological and traumatising life changing events are what drives triggers that will eventually lead to addictions and egos. They all have different sets of conditions that can target an array of different moments. Depending on the source of the trigger will depend on how and where you may be triggered. Social events like holidays, birthdays and celebrations can target childhood traumatic moments that have affected your growth since the event. Smells, voices, certain phrases, and ideologies can be linked to a variety of circles such as parents, social groups, education, and work. However, all triggers can and will be interlinked across a range of different past experiences and as we look at the individual, they all have their own story to tell. If in a single event people were witness to a moment that created a trigger and was attached to everyone, the burden they carry will not be the same as the others. Their experience means the way they digest and understand the energy will all depend on the ability to recognise their own core principles. You will never truly know other people's truths, living their life will only ever be their experience, as their life is unique to their own embodiment. The healing process will only ever be started when they are willing to begin.

The cultural mistake when addressing sensitive and vulnerable situations is the thought that they can understand how they felt within that moment. It is an experience that represents how our lives are unique to our creation. Never presume that their pain was totally within that moment, and not a combination of past traumatic events that are triggered and now attached to that event.

All your life choices and experiences will be with you until you die. It's the self-identity and empowerment that helps you learn and grow as a person that is fulfilling their life's potential.

Triggers can force a personality to change, an image of pain in a trajectory of deceit. The way a trigger is reactive internally requires an outlet to release the traumatic emotions. A person who within a conversation or a social occasion can show signs of feeling attacked.

A transfer of energy that has triggered an internal emotion that surfaces in search for a source of blame, or a vocal expression that indicates symptoms of being personally attacked. A common occurrence for someone who has neglected an energy that controls their reactions and has survived on either the victim mentality or an expression of projection. The trigger has now surfaced under a form of manipulation to avoid themselves and push their reaction of that moment towards others. Allowing someone else to carry their problem, so for a split second they can indirectly escape their pain, only to trick the mind into an ego state of avoidance, until the next time it's triggered.

A person wanting to feel at peace, but in a society that does not offer the correct source of healing and through lack of knowledge runs with the blame, as they create an alternative motive from a triggered reaction that is the source of someone else's triggers. The avoidance of happiness shows painful past emotional experiences that now merge the events of triggers to transfer their pain across society for others to absorb the energy. The healing of triggers isn't about removing them, they are part of you.

There is a three-step process that will assist as you learn to honour the relationship of your own health and an enlightened understanding of your identity across all energies within that particular moment. Acknowledgement/recognise, understanding and accepting. This process helps support your empowerment as you digest and start to evaluate your own actions, thoughts, and situations that you participate in, knowing that the transfer of energy should never be stopped. As your embodiment grows and expands to allow the natural flow of abundance from passing through you. The triggers are unprocessed past events that are part of your life. It is only when you choose to ignore yourself that disconnected lost souls allow triggers to control their thoughts and actions, manipulating future events.

Those who search towards finding an identity, a purpose, a place of peace, will no longer let past events control their future actions. It's about the long-term commitment, removing the short-term addictive states of false fulfilment in a journey of embracing the forward movement towards an inner healing and a collective consciousness.

CHAPTER 11

EMBODIMENT

The place where it all began, the spark of your creation, a history of two families merging their DNA and experiences together to create a new life as the soul attaches to the embodiment. Even though the soul attaches at the very beginning, its personal journey started long before accepting the process of its embodiment. With this new journey a divine list of principles and goals are solely bound to the individual as it looks to accomplish them. This individualised journey is unique to you, no one will ever be able to experience, see or feel what you are about to undertake. Know that you carry a connection to a conduit of a higher wisdom linked to the divine source. As any journey starts and as you grow into this life the foundational principles of your existence must be connected to the embodiment as you look towards an identity that sees that peace that comes from within. A place of collective consciousness that vibrates across all natural parts of the planet, where you can then link and interact with the sacred language, a place of guidance and protection as you commit to this new life. A journey that entails the respect of a set of core principles, a period that once the embodiment is in harmony, they will flow through you and displays personal traits of kindness, love, care, empathy, honesty, and respect. An internal inspiration that reaches to the stars as they look to honour one of the greatest achievements that one can in this lifetime.

Our soul's contract is created from previous lives by the lessons that were learnt or ignored from those experiences. A successful past life will allow you to move forward and be open to achieving a new and essential experience in the physical form. Those who failed to achieve the contract that is bound by the soul will only end up repeating or trying to amend previous mistakes. A reference point that highlights it is an honour to be able to experience our life on this planet, a place of gratitude that we take granted and ignore our own embodiment and mental health.

We are currently approaching a period that sees stages of awakening travel throughout the world. This awakening will show across many cases the struggles and neglect of their lives and mental health. An embodiment is faced with the fact that knowing that once the contract is signed you may potentially face a vast number of conflicts and obstacles to overcome in a journey where some people will be faced with ancestry pain and restrictions that hinders their growth. Even at the easiest stages of their embodiment, before they are born, they will be faced with challenges. Working with conditions that instantly restrict the connection of their soul to its embodiment, has left large volumes of the planet in limbo until this awakening.

The importance of a family and your love for them, is the key to your growth of understanding life lessons when faced upon difficult situations. Lifetimes of abusing our purpose for materialistic wealth is now catching up.

Born into a world where people's status is designed to exist on logical programming, a system that targets individuals to assist in the growth of the economy's structure as it dictates the rules and regulations in which you are subjected to. The motion of control has predetermined the parameters of your existence before you enter this world. When faced upon welcoming a newborn into a new family, emotions can within any moment forget about the logical reality and show the true power of what love can bring to someone's life. A window that is a divine reference to acknowledging the blessings as there is more to life than carrying pain and spreading it around your loved ones, a reality that will only ever compromise the growth of their future happiness. A place of security is always about being at peace with your own thoughts and actions, not losing sight of the true meaning when respecting and honouring your family and friends.

A life changing experience that you will never be able to prepare for, the unpredictability of looking after a new life that runs through your own DNA. The process of nurturing, feeding, caring and constant steps of education, a mirror image of your beliefs in how the world exists, lessons that have been taught reflect in your personality and teachings that you will soon pass on. A mixture of emotions and timeframes where you operate outside the logical realm allowing your heart to sing as you feel the love, but short lived as an ingrained programming of teachings of how you exist in this world are taught straight from the logical playbook across society. A difficult space that struggles to identify the methods of how to offer freedom but only to project your problems.

It is not just down to the interaction in which you spend quality time with your child, it's the environment in which they are placed within and the energies of the conversation which the child absorbs, especially the most potent and overwhelming conditioned atmospheres. To an extent that if the external environment doesn't release the control of the restricted logical mindset, the child will never have the honour of being able to see the values that are divinely linked to the knowledge of freedom. The transfer of energy moulds the child's beliefs by just being present.

There are three main energies which are essential information that a newborn should be taught when understanding their own identity, and for the parents to recognise the space of child's freedom so the available respect and appreciation of the individual can create a higher understanding when they offer an unconditional platform. The knowledge of freedom will be present if a space allows someone the grace to be able to understand being in the moment.

It is before any restrictions that have been placed upon their reality. Once a conditioning format is present within their mind, to find peace you then must move towards a place of healing that releases constraints from your reality and that allows their embodiment the freedom to process and acknowledge the moment. We should never look to cause pain; freedom is always about knowing the blessings of self-awareness and being in harmony with the universe. Our mindsets projects pain as we fail to see our identity, and struggle, as there are truly little teachings on how to be at peace within your own mind.

The first energy that is at the point of creation as the soul attaches to its embodiment, is a transfer of energy accessing the history of the DNA structure filled with past events of the parents' life experiences, now has the power to flow through them. A person's past life experiences are full of different individualised realities. If they are painful or fulfilling, or have been witness to life restrictions or abundances, no matter the circumstances they are all transferred, including a variety of experiences that have either strengthened or weakened the communication of their embodiment, which directly affects their mental health. The mindset of the parents is influential and especially the energies that dominate the forefront of their reality within the two individuals. Containing different sorts of energetic moments that have either enlightened them or restricted their concept of their embodiment. Displaying qualities such as stable or unstable, strong, or disconnected, peaceful, or aggressive. They are all influential energies in which the soul now must process and learn the understanding of with the merging of two individual sources that formed the embodiment a soul is now attached to.

The energy which dominates your foresight is the most potent in which is transferred across to the new life. Any struggles that stop you from self-identifying and welcoming a caring, loving environment can soon be the burden of the child's reality. A stamp of projecting Family DNA problems only for that new life to inherit which will now be left with the task of trying to overcome those negative influential energies. A decision that the idea of solving a relationship that has problems by welcoming in a new life may give you a new perspective and a motivation to start being positive, but that does not remove the transfer of your problems onto them.

Unprocessed moments that have affected you during any stage or time within your life experience have potentially hindered the direction in which you have chosen to participate within this world. A hurt that restricts your movements and closes your personal growth in a direction that sees the pain of your reality as the controlling factor when making mental choices, can soon become attached as a burdened reality of your child.

The transfer of energy within this life will either free your mind and enlighten a path of the purest form, or burden your foresight and slow your growth until a time the individual recognises they need to heal all energetic transfer of inheritance from the DNA memory. A space of healing that comes down to the individual's honesty towards personal accountability, but in a lot of cases people are never given the chance to know what is beyond their healing. You can easily become your parents, if you admire or have a conflictual relationship, the transfer of energy can dictate that you have never been given the opportunity to identity as an individual due to the personal restraints from teachings. A situation that does not represent your life, as everyone has their own identity and purpose within their embodiment. It is the divine principles and values that connect people, not the attitude that seeks to control through painful experiences.

The second lesson is to understand the value of your soul's contract. It is customised to the soul and its embodiment for certain life lessons and personal growth that will need to be achieved when accepting the journey upon entering a physical form. An evolutionary stage that works far beyond the restrictive foresight of an individual that survives on pain and seeks to gain control while avoiding the necessary lessons that need to be learnt and understood. Lessons of the evolutionary stages are never about the confined space of logic but the faith to move with freedom and wholeness towards a place that is connected to the divine source. We are here to experience the feeling of witnessing a gratitude that allows the power to run freely through us and access a network of unlimited unconditional potential.

The end goal is always about fulfilling your contract. It is hard for the current logical mindset to even process the thought, never mind participating in and connecting your own conduit of enlightenment that has access to a place of opening new doors to a divine understanding. This path is available to all of us, but not without healing and fulfilling a place of peace. Any stagnant controlling energies will prevent your growth or personal foresight to a path of enlightenment. Our lessons that need to be learnt within the contract are preparing the next step of evolving through the stages that eventually provide the gratitude of being given the greatest honour you can experience in a physical form. The first item on the list is honouring yourself, your embodiment, and the respect for your identity. A motion that requires the sacred space of peace comes from within. Everyone's list is different, you may be here to reunite with a loved one, learn an essential skill, or be part of a family. It is divinely timed to your journey, and you must recognise yourself to know that all the answers to the list are from within.

A healing process of oneness has gone unchecked and has started the dismantling of a karmic era in which we will now be faced with the task of taking our restricted conditioned reality back to a basic teaching of recognising values within core principles. Our soul's contract will be filled with basic lessons of healing and respect, for understanding the purpose within this life and the next. Each contract will be linked across a variety of past life experiences. Lessons that you failed to understand, past life actions that removed a critical part of them and eventually lost their identity and respect for others.

The relationships of connected souls are always destined to cross paths, even if the moment goes unchecked, a transfer of energy will be complete. The contract isn't just readily available to complete. Your mindset and routines will place you in different situations that allow you the opportunity of being able to participate in life events. A test of character and gratitude will always be on display when determining the results, no matter if you've accepted or rejected the lessons of your spiritual growth. This moment or any moment you were always destined to be judged. A place of disconnect will hinder and determine an outcome that you may never place yourself in a space to be able to learn the lessons that you agreed to try.

The principle of accountability and responsibility are much more than having values and gratitude within this life, it is linked to the judgement of how you enter the next life. Part of the soul's contract is the integration of the sacred knowledge of freedom and the personal identity of evolutionary progress towards the core principles that are obtained with honour. The participation of allowing healing energies to enlighten your embodiment is the peace of acceptance, which identifying your existence to gaining knowledge of a higher wisdom. Our journey requires the complete synchronisation of understanding that accepting peace will surround yourself with supporting energies and placing yourself in situations that align to the vibrational frequency of your soul's attachment to its contract.

If you ignore your happiness, you are ignoring the grounds and the terms which you accepted upon arriving in this lifetime. Times of healing will always involve struggles and reflecting on emotional and painful traumas that have prevented the blessings of internal and external growth. It is no excuse to hide away from moving forward, re-establishing the creation of a positive attitude in a direction you seek will realign supportive energies that match the divine timing of your healing.

Thirdly is power of the universe and when we are welcomed into this world, it is surrounded by a moment of divine timing, and you will only ever enter when the energies of the universe are in total harmony to your soul's contract. A language of acknowledgement that you have accepted the journey and now it's your time to honour it. The energies that we experience and are influential to our journey as they are the balancing qualities of the universe, a unique stamp of concentrated personality traits that align with certain energetic transfers and how they directly influence you during periods of your life.

The energies at the time of birth simultaneously separate and create a divine timing moment, releasing the combined attributes that are supported by the growth of the divine feminine and allows the progress of a transformative state as it creates a new unique identity of a child, which holds its own individual characteristic of an energetic relationship with the atmospheric cosmic qualities. The universe has now set the tone for how energies will influence the newborn life, their journey of understanding a life's purpose. A nurturing capacity of both parents will now be required to be present as the soul tries to understand its embodiment.

The energetic stamp from the universe is our biggest influence across all lifetimes. When we are willing to listen and learn about the deepest part of our embodiment it will help support and direct our life as we embrace our journey between different energetic influences that are forever changing and evolving. It is a reference point to health, healing, exercise, diet, career, family, education, wealth and much more. Our lessons are always evolving with the energies of the collective universe.

A journey that started many lifetimes ago has now connected to a new signature as it moves forward to try and understand the valuable lessons it must learn and experience. You can turn to the universe for guidance when trying to understand your personal life's journey. It can highlight areas that will challenge you, enlighten you and cover you in a certain energy of a particular area that is critical to your life. Astrology and monitoring the stars is and always will be our guide to this lifetime and next. To embrace this part of your embodiment you must look inwards to see outwards. A collective network that supports life.

We are in a world where we must understand our families DNA and memories, our soul's contract that depends on how we performed in previous lives and the energetic stamp of our creation from the universe. Three qualities that can only truly be understood when you identify in the moment, an embodiment that does not seek to control others, but to look inwards to see that their light shines outwards. A soul always attached at the origins of the creation; a life cannot survive with the completion of a soul to the physical form. Every feeling, idea, and reality through the period of growth as the mother is pregnant will already have imprinted a wide range of transferred experiences onto the child, and as they enter the world, they are now piecing together a reality in which the atmosphere has influenced their growth and how they interpret the world.

No matter what type of emotions and feelings the mother is experiencing, the effect in which the energy is transferred will influence the type of reality the new life may be required to carry throughout their time, as the experience becomes part of their memory. Unprocessed moments of negative energy that create blockages throughout will be transferred across to the child. The period connected to the mother influences the type of energies the child is born under.

As your heart beats today, within this moment, you may find yourself lost, having detoured away from your purpose if the energies do not align to your inner guidance. Reflection on stages of your personal journey and areas of restricted growth requires an honest and truthful search for lessons and teachings that formed your childhood memories. Ignored and removed, a reality bound by pain, but within that darkness lies a deep knowledge of how to heal. We always look to the source of problems when healing the deepest wounds. Reengaging a lost line of communication that created the platform of your ideologies and opinions is one of many branches that will assist an internal search for peace.

The blessings of knowing your parents can provide empowerment as you progress and move towards an understanding of their individual stories, a sacred line of transferred wisdom that should focus on the appreciation of life but indirectly causes a digestion of inherited problems that you may struggle to decipher. As you look towards your own personal actions it is important to recognise the origins of a personality profile that does not feel natural. The presence of your parents is instrumental to the evolutionary acceptance of establishing the energies that created you. A journey that left untouched, or the lines of communication broken, can place yourself in an atmosphere that prevents any internal blessings of appreciation. A character of one's soul must align to the values of the divine core principles, but as we look at the parents and their relationship to their own embodiments, they will now be judged on the respect they uphold for themselves and their own internal peace and appreciation for life itself.

The judgement is always bound by one's accountability to respect a balanced mind and appreciating the values of peace. They will always be judged with the task of how much of their past controls their actions, when making mental and physical decisions for their personal health. A daunting concept that rejects themselves and restricts their ability to choose a reality that doesn't involve their own pain. The nurturing values of nature are set on the conditions that it operates from a place of love, outside any logical conclusion. Allowing them to access an essential part of a collective empowerment.

Parents are essential to the balancing qualities of the masculine and feminine energetic collective traits. Even though everybody has the honour of allowing those energies to connect to the collective abundance of nature. Your embodiment is about honour, about embracing your character that has been given a selected opportunity to experience a physical form within this lifetime. Within the limits of your physical embodiment, you can only teach what you are, a lesson that you should never try to be someone else. Not even your parents.

The role of the parents represents the balanced environment that stabilises the existence of the universe, an opportunity of the highest appreciation that upholds teachings and looks to pass on a wisdom that has brought the values of life to the abundant nature of peace. The value of listening can be the most powerful realisation when looking to release personal burdens, an energy attached to the aura of your child's physical and mental reality. An energetic transfer of a personal life event that should never have been placed upon the burdened reality of your family or family member. A time where an accountable story that reflects on how a certain life experience caused so much heartache, can in turn release or start the healing process for those it affected. The transfer of negative energy can only be accepted by the truth, as we search for origins of its existence. It can then help clear a space for those it affected, helping them provide a direct pathway that is connected to the source's origins or the reality of the moments it was formed.

The benefits of sharing life experiences with your family creates an atmosphere of vibrational security and trust. Teaching those critical and important life lessons of being able to find a creative outlet that is available for a moment shared, stamped with the unique expression that is attached to the individual, while maintaining the utmost respect for the collective alignments. Time wasted on holding grudges and closing off your mindset for healing, easily misses the space that's available to learn and grow while attracting the blessings of love.

There are some people that never get the opportunity to interact and care for their family. The time you have is precious and the more you insist on sitting in a puddle of your pain, the less time you have available to know the value of the true meaning of life. Your beauty always starts from a light that shines from within. No matter your circumstances or the cards you have been dealt, healing operates on your own time and even though a family helps the healing process, those who seek to find peace without the honour of having that space available, there are always ways for you to heal the deepest of wounds. No one is left without a healing outlet. It is always up to the individual to take responsibility for their life and to know that help is always available.

In difficult spaces where people are faced with circumstances where family members have passed on or haven't been given the opportunity to spend time and appreciate their origins. They will now be required to search for alternative methods of healing, a space that should never go unnoticed. Everyone deserves to feel at peace, knowing that whatever situation you find yourself in there is always a pathway to self-identify. Knowing yourself and recognising your journey will support you when you are faced with emotional events from the past, surrounding yourself with a spiritual family will help you access information that is important to the expansion of your journey.

Our embodiment is always about learning and the life decisions we make are full of experiences that can shape our future, adapting and changing our approach to the external environments can be challenging. Welcoming a new life into the world, now potentially changes your stance from how you learn to survive, to becoming a teacher that chooses to expand their family. A spiritual identity for a soul's journey of being a student is all about honouring the divine connection to your life, when faced with life changing events. A teacher is not only responsible for their own self-identity but now must hold space for two souls to identify, separately. A realisation of supporting an individual as they grow into their embodiment and our personal internal growth as we allow peace to shine through our aura, is connected to an internal wisdom that shines from within. Healing at the deepest levels, knows that your embodiment is never about controlling others, but moving towards a divinely guided consciousness that offers peace, and sees individuals for who they are. How we cope with struggles and difficult spaces should never be transferred onto those who are under your watch, as all projected action removes the ability to recognise them and soon confuses the boundaries between your life and theirs. An action that removes personal accountability and expects others to carry their problems.

Knowing who you are helps provide a space that understands empty unsolved issues. The reassurance of being at peace will divinely guide you towards an intuitive instinct that provides an aura to attract energies during periods of healing. When you look towards your parents, it's never about blame or excuses. They are mimicking a control factor that drives their mindset, one that potentially has driven the teachings of family problems for many generations. As we approach an era that sees a new world, a rebirth of humanity. We will find that instead of inheriting a conditioned reality, we are welcomed and blessed into a space that is divinely balanced within your heart and the universe. A place where peace comes from within.

CHAPTER 12

EMPOWERMENT

The start is not defined by a singular moment, or an action of realisation, but a journey that is forever evolving as we are now faced with the harsh reality of past consequences that humans have brought upon themselves, and mindsets that have been disconnected from the divine blessings of life. As you evolve and reflect on your own imprint of the past, it should always be compared to the core principle of honour. The lack of empowerment will only survive by being able to target and instigate false realities, to draw on other people's power, in a stage of your life that highlights weakness. A shadow of manipulation is a belief that whatever is lurking in the darkness must be filled will a source of fear, a controlling factor of your reality that distances itself from approaching any difficult and vulnerable spaces of personal self-awareness. Due to the lack of empowerment as the stains in which the consequences control your internal beliefs. A narrative of conditioning that it is easier to remove yourself and become emotionless to survive in the world with no identification.

Personal traits that dominate the conversation of your internal struggles will hold a blanket of a restrictive desire to move away in the fear that it will only become worse. The damning attack on your health smooths the growth and halts any ability to search for internal peace, while the repetitive default behaviour of continuing to place yourself in situations that only ever display the beacon of pain. A direction that can operate within the parameters of the economy, to be able to maintain a job, eat and sleep, a false bubble of hope does not require you, or need you, to have any empowerment of self-awareness, as a spreadsheet only performs with numbers. A critical and essential stage of understanding the purpose of your life, while surviving with the outlined requirements of interacting with society.

The complete disconnection of being present in society will only hinder the growth of your healing. An environment in which one obtains the habits of ignoring their own mental and physical health, should always know that in those moments of transferred energy that there is wisdom of the deepest healing, if you're willing to look past your restrictive desire to avoid and start recognising a world beyond. A status of empowerment can replace the overwhelming struggle with vulnerable interaction and painful events.

The lines in which communication is constructed should never change the way your character holds values of core principles. Difficult situations are always a test of the personal values you believe. During any time of healing, the transfer of an interaction will always determine your empowerment with an energetic outcome. A person who enters a conversation that is listening to understand and not listening to respond will show signs that they are able to maintain an emotionally stable position while gaining access to a wider range in their state of control.

To lose control and zone in on a trigger will remove any space that's available to digest and reflect on other parts of the transferred information. Triggers hold a defensive stance in how your mind processes and welcomes information. A lack of empowerment disregards any alternative view that is parcelled with the translation of the interaction.

Conversations and exchanges will always involve multiple different avenues and sources that contribute to the atmosphere of the energy. A mindset that has struggled to process the painful events that dominate the forefront of their mind will enter all exchanges with a restrictive controlling umbrella of an inflicted ideology that has been emotionally charged and attached to their personality. The conversations between someone who holds a vulnerable emotionally charged state, struggles to identify the blessing of their environment, and will surround their reality with the influential controlling energies of past experiences. Activating a beacon, displaying a message that they are always searching to attract the attention of being subjected to the external environments of others. A stage that exchanges the constant reality of people targeting others as they struggle to find peace from within. A person who is randomly triggered and attacks individuals, has lost their empowerment to participate within the world and has the inability to be at peace in their own mind. They are desperate to avoid and need a release of the uncontrollable expression that holds certain aggressive qualities, as they aim to project.

A positive attitude of a conversation can halt and create boundaries in which people look to avoid the pain they carry, as their reality only knows that projecting onto others is built into their defensive default reaction. They will look for certain energetic traits and weaknesses in others, in a mindset they have lost the ability to self-identity and struggle to understand their actions, while transferring their problems onto others, the receiving party is now potentially faced with carrying their burden.

Everyone at some stage struggles with the ability to understand their mind, it's a sign of the constant conditioning the modern-day society is subjected to. A person who expresses negative forms of projection is in turn expressing their pain, the judgement of avoidance is never as easy as walking away.

You do gain empowerment by placing yourself in a positive and high vibrational environment that offers a space to expand the enlightenment of your embodiment. This is not always practical and can never always be guaranteed. The healing of others isn't always about avoiding people that are showing symptoms of being in pain, but when an exchange is present, empowerment doesn't allow them to project, but to offer them a space and expressing the burdened reality in an alternative release within the conversation. The idea of triggering someone, only shuts down the conversation and doesn't empower anyone that participates in a closed off reality afterwards.

Empowerment is always available, it's the knowledge of kindness and love, while understanding the space between the conversation.

We are always presented with moments of knowledge if you have the enlightenment experience of offering a space. It's not the act of avoidance that provides the wisdom, as the world now needs everyone to be able to offer a space and appreciate the moment. A single act of kindness is powerful enough to change the direction or to release the burden on someone's foresight, even for a moment, leading to avenues that can change their perspective and enlighten someone's day.

A true path of empowerment starts with acknowledging the deepest form of healing. Wounds that have held and contained your growth due to the conditioning, ideologies, fear, or lack of knowledge of how to find peace. A statement that involves accepting past experiences and realigning your thoughts and actions that are supported by the divine vibrational constructs of the harmonic balances within nature.

A person who is constantly surrounded by the negative aspects that forces them to release internal focus and to remove their identity will draw upon habits of laziness, carefree, negativity and display traits of anger, stress, anxiety, aggression while also carrying physical displays of pain. Society has never taught the true value of the knowledge of freedom, so the logical response is to fight against themselves, an internal conflict where there is never a winner. An attitude that is ingrained in their personal habits has created a safe zone in which they operate as they continue to fight against internal struggles. A safe zone lacks the ability to sustain a motivation and look beyond what they know, forcing a restrictive ideology of a carefree attitude that is a lonely place to be. It pushes away open gestures of kindness in the idea that the end product will only lead them to a place of pain.

When we look upon healing, the only one that can stand up and ask for help is the individual that knows the depth in which it circulates around their mind. Part of empowerment is to know that the core principle of the blessing across the universe does not heal mental traumas overnight. It's a nurturing, caring and honest journey that to find the light from within is to share the moment of enlightenment, it is how we respect others that gives you the gratitude of welcoming a loving caring quality. The idea of trying to heal someone goes against the freewill of identification, but within your empowerment you can provide an energy that welcomes them to heal, a process that will only ever start when the individual is ready.

The stabilisation of your routines can walk the trials of a reality to open the windows of observance, it is with your empowerment that daily routines and habits contain little reference points that lead to abundant moments of understanding. The challenge of processing so much stagnant emotional blockages has to be supported by a higher method of honour, it is with knowing that your daily routines ground your emotionally charged reality and send little message of reassurance and gratitude to your subconsciousness mind that even though you can't see the outcome you can start the recognising an honest place of self-care and wellness.

Emotional honesty is painful, to digest the repetitive behaviours of trying to work out the relationship of your mind, it will need supportive external sources that can offer a place of self-care, self-love, wellbeing, and freedom to be at peace in your own environment. Knowing that this journey of healing should never be done alone. Finding groups that offer a place and encourage you to express a creative outlet of an internal light, can open many new avenues and doors of self-care and internal control with how you manage the flow of energetic transfers.

The journey of healing the deepest wounds will always be changing and evolving. Your identity and your ideologies of surroundings and people can and will change every time you reach a point of enlightenment, or even the burden of realising energetic theories of personalities that has formed the way you actively participate within society. It is a constant step by step process of repointing and grounding your beliefs as you direct yourself through the methods of personal wellbeing. The more you dedicate to your purpose the quicker you will change direction, as those who have restricted their foresight of identity will always be challenged by their willingness to accept change. Empowerment is never about how many times you are willing to accept change, but accepting change for the right reason, the relationship between rules and regulations forces you to change but it's empowerment of the internal change as you look towards fulfilling the higher purpose of your embodiment.

Healing is always done when the energy and the time is right. A reliable source of friends never judges the way people heal or evolve, but to know that the path they walk depends on them. As you evolve you may seek to find alternative methods of healing, changing the direction and welcoming in a new set of friends that offer an alternative space, is about expanding your mind of awareness. It has never been about a false reality of a competitive attitude, but true wisdom falls within the knowledge of what it really means to respect someone, as people are programmed to judge, they fail to see the true beauty of what a life can offer. The balancing abundance of the universe is built on the knowing that respect is always present no matter the circumstance or the position in which your opinion takes you. Knowledge and lessons are always available if the individual is willing to listen and learn.

We are conditioned to repeat the looping traits in an objective that stabilises the economy, a behavioural pattern that you only must research history to know the lessons of past mistakes are never truly understood, but the ability to ignore provides the release of all freewill for others to profiteer. Relying on your own repetitive mindset to focus on the short-term ideology of your looping behavioural habits doesn't allow for an internal process of breaking down the energies and actions of the events. Ignoring mistakes is avoiding your own accountability and responsibility in a self-sabotaging attitude that has never been taught the true ability to welcome the feeling of a divine connection to the universe. It is with that connection you will experience love, a wholeness that welcomes the true qualities of being able to feel and experience emotions.

Situations that are relative to your healing require a range of environments. The growth of your mind will always play witness to the transformation of your personal attitude and traits. There are three essential areas that support the internal process of acceptance and accountability. Firstly, the ability to listen, instead of being triggered and closing your mind in a reality that only wants to hear your pain. Listening is about acknowledging, an allowance of letting the energies flow through you. Creating spaces that welcome people to listen and to be understood, a power that encourages the expansion of your knowledge and identifies a space that starts as it helps breakdown and read other people's energies and intentions. Separating your internal ideologies to those who are expressing theirs, a critical part of interacting with others while building on the relationship of your personal journey. A reality that is active throughout every moment of a group's expressions, such as talking to friends, meetings at work or even allowing children to express their creative outlets and blessed minds.

Secondly is expression through a creative outlet, this is all about embracing your embodiment and participating in a free flow exercise that allows the natural qualities of the earth to run through you. Lifting your vibrational auras to a place of release, letting go and feeling at peace. Singing, dancing, painting, playing musical instruments, any natural atmosphere that frees your mind and allows the internal glow from your light to shine. Simple acts of expression like talking about your day in front of your family create a reliable relationship of truth with expression, without projecting.

Thirdly is the time of personal self-reflection, removing yourself from the energies of other people while allowing yourself to sit and digest the events of how the transfer of energies were interchanged. Peace comes from within when you're able to be present in the mind and accepting a moment in silence. Releasing and removing all external influential personalities, good or bad, but identifying that honouring yourself is not driven by other people's opinions or choices. A knowing that the true strength of mental health is the relationship of your mind and your body that is connected to the ability to be at peace within your own thoughts.

It is only in a logical interpretation of a drawn-out pathway that requires avoidance and prevents a soul from connection to the larger part of life.

These individual but collective parts of healing will indicate and highlight the qualities of being able to produce a space and honour the energies that are present. The creation of opening and closing the forever evolving conditional spaces will eventually bring your attention to a higher knowing of what it means to be present with the divine flow of an unconditional source, the moment your life understands that it is okay to be at peace.

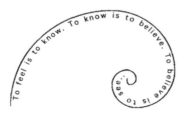

Empowerment is always present and always available, even if you don't personally recognise the strength of holding yourself accountable, your soul will always search to communicate important messages throughout your daily routines. The struggles of moving in a direction of realigning your values needs to be nurtured, the projection of a positivity can manifest spaces and moments of realisation. Manifestation is within the same mental grain that is indicated in your values of gratitude when praying, a place that looks beyond what you are trying to avoid recognising. A feeling of knowing that in your beliefs you can see.

The bigger picture in the world of manifestation is attracting energies that resonate to a high frequency of a complete oneness, but during times of healing we may concentrate our focus on the short term. Building up our confidences in times of fear or moments that lack strength, to provide and encourage by surrounding your auras with a welcoming empowerment source. Potentially activating an internal power deep inside and raising the values of your subconscious to the surface, facing your fears or situations that dominate a narrative of conditioned consciousness is always about believing in yourself. Short term manifestation is to redirect habits, conscious beliefs and routines in a direction that moves you closer to a gratitude of self-awareness.

The daunting task of trying to make changes is difficult. You've potentially formed a mental review on measuring the efficiency of your participation in avoidance. The character building of self-identification is essential as you learn to take small steps of manifestation, the true body of efficiency is to filter through the positive and negative aspects of your world. Recognising one trait per day and holding yourself accountable is a positive step towards the underlining respective core principles of self-awareness and self-care.

The truth is a rare gem nowadays, everyone puts a spin on their reality and adapts the truth to suit their situation. Surrounding yourself with people who see the truth and recognise the blessings in the world will help support your own individual journey of digesting parts of a conversation that holds value. Friends and family that struggle with processing the relationship with their mind will try and indirectly attach their truth of deception onto your beliefs. The only way to approach this situation is by working on your own health. Your mind, body and soul are the purest forms of finding a reliable source and recognising key moments to hold yourself accountable. When you unearth the truth, you're also honouring the true potential of your embodiment and recognising the value of your journey.

Little habits of terminology and selective wording can trigger a place of disconnect. Words like want, need, can, used for negative intentions will remove any ability to see the truth in your life.

The same applies for certain victim mentalities, the pain of healing is too much, so their truth is adapted to suit a situation where they can gain the most attention. A place of avoidance is only making the process of understanding the truth much harder overall.

CHAPTER 13

NEW BEGINNINGS

With every ending there is always a new beginning. The world that we know has accelerated its energies of imbalances due to the aligning sources that have called time on our current trajectory. We are currently entering a stage that is going to highlight recent changes, a platform that is going to be divided across two different directions. As we move away from the democracy umbrella, those who have hidden their intentions through deceit and profited under the framework of democracy will start to show their true colours as they seek to have a dominant control. The alternative will move away from control and for those individuals that understand life, kindness, and forgiveness will allow them the freedom, as they work towards building a community that honours the planet, a natural alignment as it moves towards a place of harmonic balances within their own mind.

The biggest task and problem you'll face this lifetime is words. They are used and manipulated to project control, deceit, and mental health issues. A person who has fallen subject to the controlling factors of others, is always bound by the words that have addressed that situation. It is easy to manipulate and sell a concept that makes you realise all personal freedoms of being comfortable within your own embodiment. We look at conversations that hold little value and have dramatic effects on our health, as the truth is buried deep within the lies of an image that is displayed within the framework, as it attaches any control you have to an addictive state of the materialistic world. Joined and accompanied by a mental image that suffocates people's freedom as they are stuck within the compounds of a disconnected reality.

Your health and wellbeing are the future of unlocking a potential that grants you the space of seeing the world for what it really is. An awakening that will move away from control and become one with the planet. A foresight that doesn't concentrate all its energy on the negative but sees the sun through the clouds and moves towards a connected reality that is directly linked to nature. People's footprints are emotional charges, wasteful and destructive, with a mindset that takes its example straight from the workings of the economy. Dedicating their life to the design framework of a controlled reality that is now going to abandon them with no place to go. An attitude that never saw the value of your mental and physical health. Their status of control has been identified and attached to the karmic imbalances of the universe.

Who would have thought that the key to your life is by recognising that you have feelings and emotions. A divine reality that opens a whole new world of being able to see yourself for the first time. Finding your identity and its silhouette in nature is a divine right, as you look to honour the core principle of the universe's energetic alignments. The harmony of being able to be present and enjoy the moment, allows the expansive relationship of your creativity to blossom through all divine times. It is the love and honour of your embodiment that knows with every beat of your heart you can experience the magic that's available when you look within. A door that leads to the collective network which is only accessible by the innate ability of self-empowerment, an acknowledgement that knows the importance of your mind and mental health.

Karmic justice is rewarded when you look within and find peace. Moving away from fear and being tricked by themes that are hidden within a mirage of certain terminologies like equal, perfect, want, while speaking the truth when looking at the umbrella atmosphere of democracy and the economy. The transfer of energy is the topic of your life. Every conversation, interaction, dietary habits, self-care, education, your relationship with nature, the list is endless, but your identity is only truly available when you place yourself in a space that recognizes the truth within the transfer of energy and how it can either enlighten you or restrict you.

We are entering an era of healing, a transitional period that will support the collective consciousness for generations to come. The healing and self-accountability of your own happiness and health can be the legacy for change. A journey that won't happen overnight, and for some it may take a lifetime to be comfortable with past actions, but it's your relationship to peace and the fulfilling moments that will support the internal growth as you move towards an enlightened embodiment.

Every chapter of this book has a divine meaning. We have covered little of the surface energy that will support you during times of healing and wellbeing. Your intuition and empowerment will manifest spaces that will centre your consciousness to places of gratitude and humble new beginnings. As your destiny has never been about living someone else's dream or life, the pain and hurt you carry suits an ideology of other people's conditioned reality. When someone paints your picture, it will always be the drums of a confined framework, a picture that controls your imagination as you project opinions and objectives out into the world for others to digest.

Daily decision making will be the foundation of moving forward, knowing that your diet isn't driven by addictive states or a carefree attitude, but about embracing the circle of life and knowing the qualities of the transfer of energy. Identifying your daily routines and areas of addiction is always a wonderful place to start, within that moment it is your choice to hold yourself accountable and make the change. An attitude that will either embrace your existence or reject the idea and place your ideology deep within restrictions of avoidance. The change is linked to the relationship between your identity and your mind.

As you enter and leave spaces it highlights the need for self-awareness by recognising how you evaluate the conditions, a process that should never be by categorisation or judgement. Any space where you categorise individuals removes your ability to identify yourself or others. An open mind reads the energies instead of drawing on predetermined conditioned realities of judgement. Categorisation encourages attitudes that target and can distance themselves from the moment while attaching themselves to personal traits of selfish, arrogant, and passive aggressiveness, all symptoms of being triggered from an internal space of disempowerment.

Placing yourself in a position that moulds the narrative of your conditioned reality does not attach a balanced relationship with friends. Feelings and emotions are about having a joyful and upbeat personality that is allowed to laugh and enjoy life. The idea of peace should inspire an intuitive personality that sees the blessings in life, attracts love and welcomes all positive and abundant opportunities.

You will always be presented with making decisions and as you reflect on past actions, it is the value of respecting yours that is presented with the true understanding of forgiveness, a topic of identity. A place of solitude where it will only ever be available when you look from within and understand your embodiment and your mental health. Your independence is difficult if you've never been offered a space of self-love and self-care, two important qualities that are divinely linked to accountability and responsibility. Change is now upon us, and your relationship with technology is destined to be judged, a period where technology has controlled society, but as healing starts, the space of knowing that it is here to support us and not control us.

Awakening and stages of enlightenment are tiring, a transfer of energy that has never been able to flow freely through but with that moment has operated under a release of control. It is important to find a reliable state of grounding and self-care. As you clear a stagnant state of control and move towards a period of dedication, you will find that education and experiences are an assertive way of being diverse in your healing. Welcoming a supportive link of communication that highlights areas of reliable information is all part of committing to yourself.

We are now entering a time where I will close this space. It has been an honour to share these teachings with you. A time where if you can see the light that shines from within you, you can move towards a period of wellbeing that can take positive steps forward, as you look to fulfil your life's potential and your soul's contract.

So as the sun rises and the sun sets, the next time you close your eyes this space will be divinely closed.

Peace, Love and Light,
Daniel Mirfield

ABOUT THE AUTHOR

Daniel has been aligned with animals and trees and attuned with the healing power of nature ever since he was a boy. Growing up in country England allowed him the time and freedom to play and explore the world around him in great detail. He currently resides in NZ after living in Australia for many years, always being drawn back to a natural setting after some city life.

It is in nature where Daniel's natural healing abilities shine. Combining a family history of ancestors connected to spirit with his own personal journey, has resulted in a man who is wise beyond his years.

A healer, a channeller, a connector to nature, Daniel is a sage for modern times. This is his first book, created to help a confused world learn to find their true authentic self and align to nature, even if you live in a big city like most of us do. He will help us heal and recover from stress. This book will be a blessing to help us all find the peace that comes from within.

Printed in Great Britain
by Amazon

19232232R00109